FOREHAND DRIVE

Forehand Drive

BY

MAUREEN CONNOLLY

AS TOLD TO

TOM GWYNNE

1957

MACGIBBON & KEE

LONDON

First published 1957

MADE AND PRINTED IN GREAT BRITAIN BY
THE GARDEN CITY PRESS LIMITED
LETCHWORTH, HERTFORDSHIRE

LIST OF ILLUSTRATIONS

PART ONE

CONQUEST

CHAPTER ONE

IN MANY WAYS this book may offer a strange story—a story not always easy to tell; because it is not easy to plumb the depths of a troubled soul. I have always believed greatness on a tennis court was my destiny—a dark destiny, at times, where the tennis court became my secret jungle and I, a lonely, fear-stricken hunter. I was a strange little girl armed with hate, fear and a Golden Racket.

For me, looking back on that brief span of star-rising, star-crossed tennis years, there is one great dramatic moment when I knew this was my year, this was my hour, this was my time to become a champion. There could be no waiting. It was not the stuff of which headlines are made, but my heart knows a total stranger propelled me into the world's championship at the age of seventeen.

One might think it difficult to select this inspired moment out of a triumphant career. It isn't. Let me set the stage for you sketchily, because so many things happened.

I had come to London from America for the first time in 1952, a sun-tanned teenager, holder of the American title, but still unproved in the eyes of the tennis world, secretly tormented by self-doubts. Immediately after we landed at the airport, I was whisked to a banquet in my honour, then taken to a boxing match. Here, I was introduced from the ring—a prophetic thing, for I, too, was a fighter.

More than anything else, I wanted to see Wimbledon, that sleeping kingdom which comes alive for two weeks each year. Here was the realm of my hopes, my fears, my dreams. There is nothing like it in all the world of tennis. It stands alone, unmatched in tradition or setting, truly Olympic, with breath-taking grandeur. Even from a distance, the massive ivy-covered

3

stadium rises in awesome majesty. The impressive wrought-iron gates were like portals to paradise, and I could scarcely believe they would open for me. Time has not tarnished memory's first picture. The huge grandstand, the beautiful close-cropped grass courts, bordered by hedges, remain always an enchanted land. As long as I live, each year the sleeping kingdom comes alive, I shall be there in spirit savouring the glory, tasting the heartbreak.

Now comes the sledge-hammer series of events. I had broken with my coach, Eleanor (Teach) Tennant, who made me a champion, taught me all the tennis I knew, manipulated my mind and body with only one goal—to win! Our quarrel was bitter, leaving scars which have never healed. I was attacked in the London Press, hounded night and day by journalists and photographers— a target for hostile headlines. I was going through a siege of fibrositis—a congested shoulder condition. A section of both Press and players believed the fibrositis to be fictional, an excuse conceived in advance to cushion defeat. I had won both my Wightman Cup matches, but neither my victory over Jean Quertier nor my three-set triumph over Jean Walker-Smith had been impressive. I was on the edge of an emotional collapse.

I had managed to reach the fourth round at Wimbledon. I got there on a path paved by my opponents' errors, certainly not by my dazzling tennis. Across the court stood Susan Partridge, a beautiful English girl, a fine player. I hated her. It was a cold, controlled hatred, part of my strategy. The fear of losing—always before handmaiden to my hate—was lacking. Eleanor Tennant believed I should beat her, love and love. I had met Susan the year before at East Hampton, New York, and beaten her, 8-6, 8-6. The scores had been close, I thought, only because I had been having an off-day. Never have I been more wrong, never have I underrated a girl so much.

Tension mounts steadily at Wimbledon and on this hot, humid afternoon, with the temperature in the high nineties, the crowd worked towards a crescendo of partisanship. Even though I thought I would beat Susan, I was nervous. I knew my game was not at a peak. She, however, in that first set, was more nervous than I. The pressure was on her and the first set was shot with errors. Susan made numerous double faults and errors off the ground. Only this, plus the fact she was hitting the hard kind of ball I like, gave me the first set, 6-3.

In the second set Susan suddenly switched strategy. She soft-balled me from the very start and I returned one high lob after another. With this overhead action, the needle pains of fibrositis jabbed my shoulder cruelly. Susan was superb. A beautiful retriever, she ran down my best and hardest placements, making a series of impossible returns. My confidence cracked. Hate and rising fear were not enough. I started serving double faults. The crowd cheered each one. This was an even more searing pain than fibrositis. In America the gallery cheered for me, but here there seemed only hostility. I became certain they believed everything critical written about me. Their reaction seemed incredible in a land where tennis flourishes as in no other, where the spectator really understands the fine points of the game. Of course, I could understand why the crowd wanted Susan to win, why she deserved to be the heroine. But I could not cast myself as the villain.

I lost the second set, 7-5. The score does not reflect the mastery Susan held. As we changed courts, she was in complete command, walking easily and gracefully to the umpire's chair. With tennis players, there are little things, mannerisms, how one stands, even the way one may towel-off after a set that reflect confidence. I stopped, crouched on my haunches, my head bowed on my racket, trying to capture a moment's rest. The contrast between us was striking. I was spiritually bankrupt, physically exhausted, so weary I wondered how long I could go on.

Just as we started the third set, Susan looked across the court, her eyes meeting mine, locking for a moment, and I can remember even now that flash of confidence. She served. The rout began. After she won her service, I felt as if I were on the way out, defeat certain, discredited, unpopular, measured and found wanting on this biggest tennis battlefield of all.

When we changed courts, I walked by the players' section, building a hope in my mind, buttressing it with prayers. Eleanor Tennant would be there! She had to be! No matter how stormy our quarrels had been, she would not leave me to face this crisis alone. I sought that flashing look of encouragement, that surging extension of power which flowed from her. I needed a miracle to win and only Teach could manufacture my miracles. But as my eyes ranged the rows of faces, I knew my well-spring and inspiration was gone. I saw my mother, and she smiled, then shook her head slightly, reading my mind.

Now I was utterly alone, afraid, with a rising fear; for the first time in a major match I felt hopelessly adrift.

As we played, the crowd tripled, fervour mounted, the kill was close. The set became 4-5 in Susan's favour, the game score, 15-30. She was within two points of winning the match. I served a fault. If I double-faulted, she would have match point. For the first and only time in my career, I became almost ill with a nausea which threatened to choke me. I managed, somehow, to get my serve in, but, more remarkable still, I won the point, bringing the point score to 30-30. A low moan rose from the gallery. The crowd had eagerly anticipated Susan's getting match point. But now I was too tired to care, too scarred from the emotional lashes to feel one more sting.

The crowd leaned forward, the moment was tense, there was a hush, when suddenly, piercing the silence, a young voice rang out clear and bold, 'Give 'em hell, Mo!' I stood stunned, paused, looked and saw a U.S. Air Force boy. His face was a flash of youth, shining and glowing with friendliness. I did not know him. I have never met him. But truly, in that second I was lifted to the heights by a stranger. I smiled and said 'Thank you' in a fervent whisper.

Truth can be stranger than fiction. If it seems incredible to believe one ringing cry of encouragement can turn the tide of a hopeless match, I say only—it happened.

Confidence surged through me, a new vitality lifted me. Savage determination powered me. I looked across the court at

Susan and knew I would win. I knew it with a conviction impossible to explain. I was a clutch player, more dangerous when I was behind. I told myself this. I knew it was true. Susan was the enemy. She blocked my way. I hated her. I would move in for the kill. The pains of fibrositis were nothing. My exhaustion vanished. If my knight in the grandstand were on alien soil, so, too, was I. Only victory could bring the conquest I sought. I took the game, the set, 7-5, and the match.

There was a touch of magic and it touched the crowd. Perhaps a few heard the voice of the stranger, perhaps they sensed how beaten I was, how forlorn a figure, because their cheers for my errors stopped. They could have been aware of the tremendous uphill struggle I faced. But none realized more clearly than I that mental pain can be far greater than physical pain. I had experienced both to the hilt.

How can one write and hope the reader may believe that winning the finals at Wimbledon—the world's championship of tennis—can be anti-climactic? It was for me. I had crossed the Rubicon. For the first time in my career, I knew I could win without Eleanor Tennant. Such a thought before had been so deep in the realm of fantasy it had never seriously crossed my mind. It would have been like going on the court without a racket, unarmed, completely vulnerable.

In the short space of a few exciting days I became the second youngest winner in all Wimbledon history (the first girl since the incomparable Suzanne Lenglen to win the first time she entered). Later, I want to tell you about those matches and so much more about Wimbledon. But for me my first Wimbledon was Susan Partridge, and the voice of the stranger remains the most dramatic incident in a career crowded with thrilling matches and impossible victories.

In 1953 I became the first 'Grand Slam' champion in women's tennis, with Wimbledon, the United States, Australian and French titles mine. In victory's first full flush I was compared to Suzanne Lenglen, Helen Wills, Alice Marble. In the tournaments to come, some tennis writers flattered me by hailing me as the greatest woman player of all time—an accolade I cannot accept.

Tennis has brought me many things—international acclaim, love, heartaches, and deep tragedy. Then, suddenly, it was all over, the all-too-brief years of glory gone, but even in the bitterness and despair, following the accident which almost cost me my right leg, there was a silver lining.

Few champions leave the arena before the zenith of their career. Few depart the scene of battle with no fields left to conquer. How did it happen? What is it like? I hope I may tell my story honestly, with candour, as it happened and for what it may be worth. I tell it with mixed emotions, but if ever a career could be given a caption, mine was :

'Win! Win! Win!'

CHAPTER TWO

I WAS BORN within a lob shot of three cracked cement tennis courts, but Fate's finger did not beckon until I was nine years old. No tennis player in the world could ask to be born in a nicer city than San Diego, California—famed for its equable climate. Tennis can be played eleven months of the year, usually under a warm sun, and this is a prime reason why Southern California has produced so many champions.

My name was to be Robert. This choice was made on the basis of pre-natal speculation by my mother's doctor, who inclined an educated ear, heard a lusty heart-beat, and declared this could emanate only from a baby boy. There was, it appeared, no area of doubt in this oracular forecast, and only masculine names were considered.

For the doctor, I was a boomerang baby. He had a nice sense of one-way humour and his speciality was teasing the nuns at Mercy Hospital. My arrival provided an opportunity for retaliation and the sisters of the cloth banded together and made him acutely aware of his error. I was trouble in Babyland. Mom had no name for me; the birth certificate could not be completed, and perhaps the doctor became weary of hearing 'How is SHE?' and 'What a darling little GIRL!' at last, Maureen Catherine was chosen. The doctor, however, was not altogether wrong. In many ways, I was to grow up like a boy.

My father was Martin Connolly, a lieutenant commander in the U.S. Navy. He was the athletics officer at the Naval Training Station, and although he had a fine engineering background he likewise had been an accomplished athlete during his days at the Naval Academy at Annapolis. Tennis was not his game, but perhaps he gave me an athletic inheritance. He had been an outstanding boxer, a top baseball and football player, as well as a hockey star, his favourite sport. My parents were divorced when I was not quite four years old. My last memory of my father came when I was ill. He looked down at me, smiled and told me he would buy me a chocolate sundae, topped with nuts, when I recovered. It seems odd such an incident should remain fresh in memory over the years and become my clearest mental picture of my father. We never heard from him, never knew where he might have gone. Years later, we believed he had been killed in an accident. News of the accident, long after it had happened, was relayed to us in fragmentary detail by friends, but it could not be checked or confirmed.

My mother was born in Helena, Montana, deep in the heart of the cattle country, and although she was a fine horsewoman music was her first love. As a child she showed great promise as a pianist, but her fingers did not grow properly and she could not span an actave. Thus her great dream for a concert career died early, leaving with it a lifelong frustration; the music that was in her would never be given expression on the piano keyboard. Mom was a beautiful girl. I have a portrait of her and it is striking as only that rare, dark, dramatic type of Irish beauty can be.

Mom and I lived with my great-aunt in a red-brick house; a modest home in a modest neighbourhood. I was a 'depression baby,' as America and the rest of the world struggled in the toils of economic reverses. Money was far from plentiful, but never in my girlhood did I lack for anything I really wanted. Auntie, Mrs. Gertrude Wood, was a court matron, caring for wayward girls. She and Mom made many sacrifices, and Auntie took a firm hand in my upbringing. She is now eighty-four years old, an oak-like woman, extremely kind and generous and endowed with great common sense and logic. I owe her much. Her sharp and kindly eyes have been trained on me since babyhood.

Mother blueprinted my life early. I would achieve the artistic heights she never reached. Ahead stretched my career—dancing, singing and the piano. Although I do believe in predestination, none of this was in Destiny's deck. But according to Mom, I made a brave start. At four I was enrolled in ballet class, where Mom played the piano to help defray the cost of tuition. It was then I first displayed an exceptional ability to memorize. I was able to learn and retain dance routines with an ease bordering on the fantastic.

Eleanor Tennant believes all tennis champions have a strong streak of exhibitionism. If this be true, I was a perfect example. I was a 'ham' in infancy. In the first production our dancing class gave, the other little girls developed stage fright. But not I; at least, so Mom says. I raced about, recited their lines as well as my own, making a frantic effort to hold the show together.

Schooldays began when Mom enrolled me in a small school operated in connection with the dancing academy. I promptly became a terror, refusing to take my nap, waking up the other little girls, racing about the halls and compounding confusion. Mom was incredulous when I was reported constantly. I had been a model pupil in dancing class, but there a parental eye looked out over the piano keyboard.

My dancing career was short-lived. I was given a try-out in an advanced toe-dancing class, but lacking Mom's supervision I managed somehow to disrupt the group. Now I was through with dancing, utterly unhappy with the school; so Mom put me in the Jefferson Grammar School, near our home. Dancing remained in the master blueprint, but it was postponed until the next year, supposedly. Actually, I didn't resume dancing until some years later when I took up tap, but only as a means of improving my tennis footwork.

My singing career was equally brief. I had a husky baby baritone and I was eager to sing at school, but my teacher, hardly an operatic coach, thought I was a soprano, or at least wanted to turn me into one. This infuriated Mom, who had gone to considerable trouble to transpose songs for me in a lower key. Well, if I couldn't sing baritone, I wouldn't sing at all. Later an ineptly performed tonsillectomy impaired my vocal cords, and thus my prospects as a singer, if any, vanished.

Of course, Mom tried her best to make me a pianist. I was

exposed daily, but the inoculation didn't take. I watched the clock constantly, eager for the moment when I could race out and play. Girls? Dolls? They both bored me. When I was five, I received a lovely doll, but I had been expecting a brand-new ball, and in disappointment and rage I hurled the doll against the wall.

Now I turned to outdoor sports, and suddenly a new and wonderful vista opened in my childhood. I loved games. I had a natural flair for them. It wasn't long before I ran like a boy, threw a ball hard and straight, excelled in jumping and climbing. I became too rough and rugged for the girls and finally I was accepted on equal terms by the boys of our neighbourhood.

Horses became my deepest childhood love, and in my early girlhood, before my big-time tournament career really began, I would have thrown over tennis for horses had such a choice existed. I started with pony rides, and I could have ridden for ever if we had been able to afford it. However, it cost nothing to play with the boys in our neighbourhood and they were always eager for me to join them. In my headlong dash to the playgrounds, I passed the tennis courts daily—they were only two doors from home—but tennis held no allure. I had taken a few fleeting glances, but the players were less than expert, and the game, especially the way the girls played it, appeared utterly ridiculous.

Then came the fatal day! I was nine years old, on my way to play softball, when suddenly, for the first time, I saw real tennis. Gene Garrett, a handsome man whose game had style, was playing against Arnie Saul, an equally good player. Never had I seen anything like this! Their rallies were long, hard; their serves blistering, the net play dashing. I stood entranced. Time passed, but I did not move. Suddenly, every game I knew and loved palled. It happened just like that. The tennis virus raced through my blood. I made up my mind to become a tennis player, certain I needed only a racket in my hand to vanquish any little boy or girl in the neighbourhood.

Overnight my life changed. I haunted the tennis courts,

watched closely, absorbed everything I could, waiting eagerly for the golden moment when I might play. It was inevitable that the professional, Wilbur Folsom, who maintained a small tennis shop at the courts, should notice me. I had become as much a fixture as a net-post. Finally, Folsom spoke to me and opportunity unfolded. At the moment he had no ball boy; he was giving a lesson to two girls. Would I chase balls for him? Would I! In return he would let me hit a few later. Since then I have seen ball boys in all parts of the world, but none matched my zeal on that summer's afternoon.

The lesson stretched on for ever. Neither of the girls impressed me. I was certain I could beat them both. At last the session was over. Now I was alone with Folsom, impatient to get into action, ready to show my quick mastery over this fascinating new game. Folsom gave me a racket, showed me how to hold it, then supplied the balls. I was poised to slam over a drive just as I had seen Gene Garrett and Arnie Saul do it. Alas, I was doomed to crushing disappointment. The ball simply would not go over the net. I couldn't co-ordinate. I stood there angry, baffled, completely frustrated, and I'm sure no tennis player in the world ever made a more inauspicious début than I.

Any championship career has foundation-stones. Mine were slavish work and driving determination. Even at the outset, Folsom became aware of my burning inner fire, because either in pity or compassion he volunteered to give me a few pointers. In return I would become his ball boy. (At least, I excelled there.) He suggested I come over the next afternoon, but I was on the courts the next morning long before his shop opened.

Now my unchallenged position in the tight neighbourhood athletic social structure (masculine division) meant less than nothing. I would become a tennis star! There was no middle ground; only the top would suffice. Thus, in the next two months, I became Folsom's shadow, a whirling dervish as a ball boy, the most eager pupil he ever had. Finally, he decided to have a talk with Mom about my tennis. This new and burning love of mine for tennis came as a complete surprise to her. She had no inkling I had been playing tennis. Perhaps even then, I kept my thoughts and dreams bottled tightly inside me. Seeing my enthusiasm, Mom offered immediate help. Folsom suggested she buy me a racket and a course of lessons.

I was launched! Mom bought me a $1.50 racket—now one of my most treasured possessions—and arranged for me to get two formal lessons a week at fifty cents each—truly a bargain compared with the $25 an hour the Hollywood movie stars pay. I was left-handed, I still write with my left hand, but I'm almost ambidextrous. One afternoon Folsom noticed me trying to hit a few balls with my right hand, and wisely, because so few good players are southpaws, suggested I switch over. This transition was extremely difficult, but certainly worth the struggle. I need not tell you I played and practised every available moment.

My tournament career, to use the phrase lightly, began when I was ten and a half. La Jolla, a beautiful seaside suburb of San Diego, holds an annual playground event, and at Folsom's suggestion, and with Mom's approval, I was entered in the thirteen-year-old-and-under division of the girls' singles. Naturally, I would win. The possibility of defeat simply had not occurred to me. You see, I was starry-eyed even then; my confidence knew no limits. I did manage to reach the finals, but here I fell before the superior and more polished play of Ann Bissell, who was a year older than I.

I had never studied to be a gracious loser, and in my sports lexicon there were no neatly turned congratulatory phrases. I cried inconsolably on the way home, drenching Mom's shoulder with my tears. She was amazed at the depth of my feeling. After all, she explained, tennis was only a game and one must take victory and defeat with equal grace. This wisdom fell upon deaf ears, and it was then Mom knew I was no ordinary tennis player, I was no ordinary little girl, and tennis to me, even then, was much more than just a game. Defeat was unendurable; it could not be talked away by the sympathy of an understanding parent. It must be avenged!

Beating Ann Bissell became my single goal in life. Towards

this one end I turned my efforts, working tirelessly, stopping only when darkness fell. The next tournament was a minor scholastic affair on my home University Playground courts, but here Ann foiled me without design. She knew nothing of my secret determination to beat her. She simply had not considered the event important enough to enter. So, playing like one of the Furies, I won my first tournament. Triumph brought no inner satisfaction at all. The champion had not been there.

Ahead loomed San Diego's one big event for the juniors—the Harper Ink Tournament—and Ann Bissell was entered! Joy and hate surged through me, for now there would be repayment on the field of battle for my defeat, there would be a glowing dividend for my hundreds of hours of practice. There were other girls in this tournament only a shade less formidable than Ann, but they meant nothing. I reached the finals and so did Ann.

As the California sun beat down on us, we were just two little girls with tennis rackets, but the contrast to a keen observer could have been striking. My very existence depended on victory. I could not lose or my world would shatter in pieces. I am sure Ann felt no such overriding emotion. I charged into combat with my $1.50 racket held as high and deadly as a warrior's lance. I can remember even now winning that first point. My ball hit the top of the net, trickled over for a sure point. This was a magic sign, an omen of victory. Our rallies were long, hard, the score always close, and if she was more polished and seasoned than I, she lacked my tireless energy, the compelling urge to dash headlong for the most impossible shot. I beat her and I tasted glory's brimming cup; it was sweet.

Disappointment came quickly when I returned to my old cracked cement playground courts. Wilbur Folsom picked me as a target—the one girl the others should strive to beat. This infuriated me. I wanted to be the hunter, not the quarry, and I looked on my victory in the Ink tournament as a stepping-stone to greater triumphs. Here I do not wish to sound ungrateful to Folsom, because he gave me a tremendous lift, and in many ways he was a remarkable man. He overcame the handicap of an artificial leg, covered the court with considerable agility, and truly was an inspiration. Perhaps he was much happier in devoting his attention and interest to a great many boys and girls rather than concentrating on the starry aspirations of one.

It was at this time I was offered a complimentary membership in the Balboa Tennis Club. I accepted, thus leaving Folsom's wing. Was I ruthless even then? Perhaps, to a degree, I was. My tennis could not stand still; I must improve at all costs, and here was an opportunity. Now, four boys, all fine players, entered my life at the new club, and each in his way improved my game. They were Ben Press, Hugh McArthur, Bob Galloway and Bob Barth—all of tournament calibre—and each went out of his way to give me encouragement and pointers, always willing to play with me. I had completed the full circle, back again with the boys, going against a harder, faster type of tennis than most girls could offer.

Slowly I was on the rise, but soon I was to come under the spell of the greatest coach in the game—Eleanor Tennant.

CHAPTER THREE

ELEANOR TENNANT is the greatest tennis teacher in the world. The fact that we quarrelled often, finally split and no longer are friends does not diminish in the least my respect for her genius or lessen the gratitude I feel. People like Miss Tennant and me, with only one driving obsession—to win—are not entirely normal in the accepted meaning of the word. History's painters, pianists, poets and generals all lived with a burning fixity of purpose. So it was with Teach and so it was with me.

Our quarrel on the eve of my first Wimbledon left me emotionally torn. It was difficult for a young girl to draw charity's veil over bitterness, to rationalize, compensate and reconcile. The newspaper stories saying she was washing her hands of me, that I was headstrong, wouldn't listen to her and now had no chance of winning, hurt deeply. Then fury took over. I had wanted to break with her before, but Mom had always held us together. Now I was through.

I am sorry the whole thing had to happen, but I no longer feel bitterness or anger. I am sorry for Teach, for what she did to herself. I think the greater share of blame lay with her, but certainly I was not blameless. I, on the tennis court, was what she had made me, and when we parted and I succeeded without her it was a heavy blow. In the mind of a young girl, right and wrong are like black and white. There are no shadings. Now, of course, I realize if Miss Tennant had not possessed her own special and unique set of qualities she wouldn't have been the great coach she was. Sometimes when I am coaching a player now, the stray thought pops into my head: 'How would Teach do it?' As an instructor, I perhaps have followed in her footsteps.

My meeting with Teach was part of the pattern of my life, part of a curious destiny, if you will. I was twelve and a half years old and in my almost bare 'trophy room' stood the Ink cup—shining and resplendent, but awfully lonesome. Now I was on the trail of bigger tennis game. Mom and I had gone to Los Angeles, where I had been entered in the thirteen-year-old and fifteen-year-old-and-under age divisions of the famous Pacific Southwest Tournament—an event which attracts the Wimbledon and Forest Hills winners.

My quest for glory was a rather well-kept secret, because not only were the tournament officials unaware of me, but there was no available court on which to practise. Mom and I, however, found a suitable training ground at Griffith Park, a public playground. I believed, of course, I needed countless hours of practice to win. It was here I met Curt and Daisy Tree, dancing instructors and tennis enthusiasts. Daisy, who was then approaching sixty but played with the verve of a girl, and I became friends, and she was impressed by my headlong charges, my furious determination to make every impossible shot.

'Eleanor Tennant could make her a champion,' Daisy said to Mom with quiet conviction. Daisy explained who Miss Tennant was, and as she painted a glowing picture of a great coach Mom and I could not believe it possible such a famous tennis teacher would bother with me. However, I had had no coach since I left Wilbur Folsom and I wasn't (and never have been) satisfied with my strokes.

Oddly enough, Daisy did not know Miss Tennant, had never seen her, but she was convinced Teach would take me as a pupil. We left the arrangements to Daisy, who radiated confidence. Just what sort of an adjective-laden prospectus she gave Teach on the phone I never knew, but an interview was arranged.

We met Miss Tennant at the Beverly Hills Tennis Club, where she was the professional. I was frightened and excited. I had never seen such lavish surroundings, and the first person I saw was the late John Garfield, the movie star. But among the expensively dressed crowd, many of whom wore the Hollywood badge—dark glasses—I knew there must be hundreds of other film celebrities.

I was surprised and awed when I first met Teach. I had expected someone younger. She was then in her late forties, a slender, graceful woman, with a smooth face tanned like old leather and topped by striking silver-grey hair. She was wearing a T-shirt and slacks.

'You must be Maureen?'

'Yes, Miss Tennant.'

'Let's hit a few. I want to see what you can do.'

Direct. No preliminaries. Fixity of purpose. That was Teach. I had expected a long conversation, but unless I had promise I was wasting her time, and that was worth $25 an hour. In this brief encounter I was struck by her compelling voice, her manner of complete domination. Mastery flowed through her. Here was a confident, supercharged personality.

At that moment I wanted Teach for a coach more than I wanted anything else in the world. Power was my forte and I had to impress her, so I resolved to hit everything hard in our rally. Was I nervous? Not when I got out on the court, because the pressure was on, and that I relished. Luckily, a high percentage of my drives were good. Teach gave me a few pointers, among them the advice not to be late with my backhand, to hit on the rise. She tested my serve, volley and forecourt play, as well as my baseline slugging.

'A twelve-year-old taught me something about teaching,' she later told a friend.

Teach used a highly unorthodox but extremely effective method with me. She believed serving is much like throwing a ball. I, a natural left-hander, did not throw well with my right hand, and Teach saw that at once. The shoulder co-ordination was not right. Instead of having me serve, she gathered up a number of old rackets and I threw them, pretending each time I was serving. This helped me at once.

I played in the Pacific Southwest and won in both divisions, but what might ordinarily have been a heady triumph now meant very little. There had been no Ann Bissell to chop down here, and more than anything else I knew my game was shot with faults, that my strokes were not right. Teach cancelled her appointments to watch me in the finals and to catalogue my mistakes.

Now the grind started. I returned to San Diego as school was in session, but I went to Beverly Hills on weekends for instruction under Teach. That summer I really toiled, but I was a long, long way from the perfect game I sought.

Two incidents stand out from that period. Teach permitted me to play in the Santa Monica tournament, held in a seaside suburb of Los Angeles, and here I disgraced myself. I reached the finals in the fifteen-and-under age division, where I met Molly Shea. It was during this match I lost my temper for the first time on a court, and I lost it with a vengeance. Even from the first day I held a racket I would become furious at myself for missing a shot, but in tournament play I had controlled myself. Now my shots were not working right, I was not playing well. I thought with all my practice my game should be dazzling, but it was far from it. I was furious at myself, and it was a mounting fury. I behaved like a little hellion, banged balls against the fence, hurled my racket and shocked the gallery. Naturally, my play deteriorated steadily, and, of course, Molly beat me.

Revenge loomed uppermost in my mind, but I never met Molly again as a junior, and when I did play her I was the world's champion and she a college student, with tournament tennis strictly a secondary interest. By then my personality had undergone a change, revenge appeared juvenile and I did not try to blast Molly off the court. (I could have been growing up!)

The other incident concerned Teach's strict orders to practise and not play, but the magic of movie stars at the Beverly Hills Club proved my undoing. I'd sneak in an occasional game with John Garfield or Cornel Wilde, but my downfall was Gilbert Roland. He's a handsome man, with a charming and infectious personality, and he's a fine player. (He beat me.) Teach caught me and I was sent home on the spot. My world collapsed.

Mom met me at the San Diego bus station, and I expected sympathy I did not get. I was wrong, Teach was right, and Mother told me to write an immediate letter of apology. Later I cried in my room, as I was to do many times after a disagreement with Teach, but I wrote the letter and she took me back. That winter, at Teach's suggestion, I took up tap dancing to improve my footwork. It did, and my dancing teacher, Joanne Thornbrook, became a good friend.

Teach changed my game completely. I still had a residue of faults, a heritage from my earliest days as a left-hander, with an accent on undercutting and slicing. Teach gave me the flat shot, which is absolutely essential to good tennis. The fine ground strokes she taught me became foundation-stones of a winning game. Different coaches have different methods, but Teach used a highly effective imaginary clock system. I stood in the backcourt and imagined I was in the centre of a large clock dial, with twelve o'clock directly behind me. I started my forehand at twelve, hit at nine o'clock and followed through to six o'clock. The backhand was just the reverse. I developed sound strokes, a power game, and later during my career, if a shot soured, Teach would bring me back to this basic bit of practice and straighten out the shot.

At first it was Teach's intention to pattern my game along the lines of Alice Marble, whom she considered to have been the world's greatest woman champion. Miss Marble's forte had been a deadly volley preceded by a 'big serve.' Going to the net after a forcing shot is perfect strategy, but at that point of my career it was not for me. My net game, a really great one, was almost impossible for me to achieve, due, I think, to an unfortunate incident when I first started playing. I had been hit by a smash when I had been at net, and this acted as a mental hurdle for a long time. However, Teach clung to the idea I might play as Marble had, but finally, as I shall explain later, she gave it up.

Tennis is a world to itself, and as in any other specialized field there are personality clashes. For Teach they were inevitable. She was always dominant, outspoken, a positive thinker at all times; she abhorred stupidity, and her likes, dislikes and opinions were considerably less than State secrets. I was caught dead centre in 'no girl's land' early in my career. Perry T. (Pep) Jones, sometimes referred to in the American Press as the Emperor of Western Tennis, has, like Teach, a dominant personality, and to say they did not always see eye to eye is an understatement. Jones, a gentleman of the old school, fastidious to his fingertips, believed young ladies should be attired in correct and demure tennis dresses. Teach was a staunch advocate of T-shirts and shorts. Naturally I did not want to offend either. Teach ruled me and my game. Jones, then secretary and now president of the Southern California Tennis Association, held rigid control over tournament invitations and expenses. Both were my friends, both interested in furthering my career, but between them my position was not always a happy one.

In one early tournament I was wearing shorts and a T-shirt —all I had—and neither garment was fashionable or expensive. Jones looked at me in horror. I might have been wearing burlap to the Royal Ball. He took Mom aside and explained with deft diplomacy that I was something less than a candidate for tennis's best-dressed ten. He implemented this opinion by pressing a fifty-dollar bill on Mom to purchase a suitable outfit. (That was really a lot of money to us.)

Later, Teach chose my clothes, on and off the court. Her taste was severe, but impeccable. Here I must add she was a very generous woman.

There was a broad background for my break with Teach, and, although I have never studied either psychology or psychiatry, I believe, to some extent, it was a curious case of my becoming Teach's *alter ego*. I worshipped her at first. She could do no wrong. Her opinions became fact for me. Her likes and dislikes became mine. I am ashamed to say there was a period when Teach supplanted my mother in my life. It was to Teach, not Mom, I looked for counsel, and if there was a divergence of opinion I was on Teach's side. However, as time went on, my submissive, Trilby-like attitude changed. I became more dominant and headstrong, and in this task force of two there was room for only one field-marshal.

Teach believed everything in my life should be sublimated to tennis. However, I liked to forget tennis occasionally, have dates and a good time. Perhaps I gave Teach some bad moments, because, as I have said, the blame did not lie entirely with her. One incident, seemingly trivial to me, resulted in a stormy quarrel. I had gone out on a double date, the car broke down and we didn't get home until dawn. Mom accepted my story as truth. Teach didn't. She not only doubted my word, but she was furious because I failed to keep a tennis date with her the next day. My young temper matched hers.

Another time I wanted to leave home and live with Teach. I was certain she wanted me more than anything else in the world. She didn't. Mom told me Teach wanted me to stay at home. I did not believe her at first. This was a sledge-hammer blow to my ego. Then Teach would complain to Mother about me, that I practised too much. As far as tennis went, I thought I knew what I needed, and it was work, work, work. I played at night as well as in the daytime, because some of my men partners worked and could play against me only at night.

Tennis, to Teach, was never a game, it was a battle, and no field-marshal mapped strategy more carefully. She scouted every formidable opponent I faced and spotted strength and weakness with absolute accuracy. She was the field-officer, I the troops, and we went into action with deadly purpose and total concentration. If Teach knew the enemy, she also knew me, and how close she might drive me to the breaking-point in practice before easing the pressure. She likewise knew, far better than I, the exact tensile strength of my game in the hardest match. Her confidence was a living, glowing thing, without limits, and she had the magic power of being able to transfer it. Lose was not a word in her tennis vocabulary, and even if she thought I might be defeated I never knew it. Then, too, Teach was a master of psychology, and I have heard part of her great success with Alice Marble was the exercise of this mental power.

My first tour gave me a chance to put into practice the new game Teach had given me. The trip, which was sponsored by Harper Ink and Perry Jones, was wonderful. Patsy Zellmer, my dearest friend and doubles partner, was to make the swing with me. I was thirteen that summer and Patsy was fourteen. We packed and unpacked dozens of times before we finally left for Los Angeles, where we joined Barbara Kimbrell, a fine player who was to be our chaperone, and Beverly Baker, Johnny Fleitz and Hugh Stewart, who also would tour with us.

We played in Salt Lake City, Denver, Seattle, Tacoma and the beautiful British Columbia cities of Victoria and Vancouver. I had always played on cement, but at Salt Lake I was introduced to clay for the first time. Then, in British Columbia, the courts were grass, which became my favourite surface.

The tennis, from the first to the last tournament, developed and retained the same pattern. I won the eighteen- and fifteen-and-under singles, and Patsy and I teamed to win the doubles in these divisions, but each time I stepped into the senior class Beverly Baker trounced me. She was four years older than I, destined to become the United States junior champion that year. (It was on this tour, by the way, that the romance between Beverly and Johnny Fleitz began. They are now happily married.)

Laden with trophies and prizes, I returned to San Diego, and now my lonely trophy had company. My tennis had improved, a bit of tournament polish had been rubbed on my game, but my attack was basically the sound ground strokes Teach had taught me. Yes, she had given me much, but, unwittingly I am sure, she had lighted a flame within me—a flame that was almost to destroy me, even as I fought my way up to the championship of the world.

It was the fierce flame of hatred!

CHAPTER FOUR

THIS IS THE STRANGE CHAPTER of my book, the dark chapter of my career. It is, I believe, without counterpart in tennis, alien to the experience of any girl I have known; no part of any past champion. I hated my opponents. This was no passing dislike, but a blazing, virulent, powerful and consuming hate. I believed I could not win without hatred. And win I must, because I was afraid to lose. The fear I knew was the clutching kind you can almost taste and smell and the spectre of defeat was my shadow. So, tragically, this hate, this fear became the fuel of my obsession to win.

I cannot say which emotion was the stronger, which drove the harder. I have seen motion pictures of my matches, long after they were played, and I looked with a cold shudder at the mask I wore—that tightly drawn face, the fixed expression, the mechanical responses of tennis etiquette. If eyes truly are the windows of the soul, I am thankful no one looked into mine. This was the real me, the little girl no one knew. As I tell this, I am reviewing a stack of newspaper and magazine clippings. They relate the rise of a sweet youngster to the pinnacle of tennis. The photographs show a 'prop smile.' Aside from the critiques, they might have been about someone else. I walked alone, telling not a living soul of my consuming passions.

No self-analysis is expert. Searching one's soul can be a trying business, but the beginning, I think, lay rooted in my spirit— temper if you will—a flashing Irish heritage. To this I added a doctrine of perfectionism. The hard core of the one destiny I believed in was that I should play better tennis than any other girl in the world. I was a suppliant before an altar. No one wanted fame, success, security, admiration and the world's championship more than I. I grew up in a home that was twice

broken, and even from the first I disliked my stepfather, Auguste
Berste, a San Diego musician whom my mother married just as
my career was starting. I missed having a father like other
girls and complained of it; perhaps this was one of the reasons
Mom married again. But I rebelled at the start. I did not want
Mom to leave me for the honeymoon and I raised a terrible
scene. I blamed my stepfather for taking my mother from me,
if only for a few days. Such is a child's mind. The marriage,
which lasted about five years, was not happy. It was punctuated
by quarrels and reconciliations, complicated by my tennis and
Berste's health. He developed ulcers and with them a personality
change. He thought my tennis career was being pushed too fast,
and there was little harmony in our home during those years. I
hesitate to include details of my mother's unhappiness, but if
I am to give you an honest picture of my life I cannot omit
them.

Perhaps I had an insecurity complex, maybe I thought tennis
would bring me everything, that it was tomorrow's only hope.
I do not know. I did not want to spend a minute away from
tennis, and so, as I told you, the tennis court became my secret
jungle. I, the hunter, stalked my prey with the venom of a
hungry tiger. Surely, you might reason, such a killer would
know no fear, and at times, to my distaste, I had been called a
killer in the newspapers. This struck too close to the truth, the
truth I wanted no one to know, but 'killer' is a stock adjective
in sports writing and 'killer in pigtails' didn't have any special
connotation for anyone except me. Yet, I knew fear—the fear
of defeat. You see, the curious coin of my personality had a
reverse side. I had to win because I wanted to be liked, and
only by winning, I thought, would I be liked.

One match which remains vivid in memory crystallized my
feeling of fear. I was fourteen years old, a dashing little girl in
a cute tennis dress, the summer sun catching sparks from my
auburn hair. Perhaps to the spectator I appeared to be a creamy
concoction of sugar and spice. The setting was the Hotel del
Coronado, a famed landmark of the Pacific, which holds an

ABOVE *Maureen Connolly with her doubles partner in Australia, Julie Sampson – a fellow Californian and one-time United States Junior Champion*

BELOW *With Julie Sampson and Lew Hoad during Maureen Connolly's first invasion of Australia*

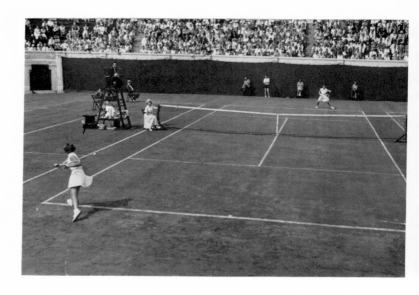

*Two action shots in Maureen Connolly's match against
Shirley Fry (far end) during the 1951 American finals*

(*Life* PHOTOGRAPHS BY PETER STACKPOLE)

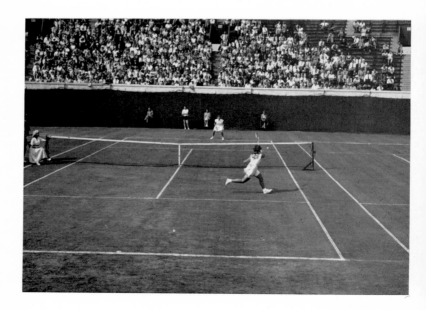

annual tournament on courts bordered by a long white beach and low, rolling waves—a truly beautiful backdrop.

Before the match I was happy, thrilled and sure of winning. I was the centre of attraction, the heroine of her home courts. Everyone, or so it seemed, was anxious to tell me what a charming and talented little girl I was, to pat me, hug me and wish me good luck. I basked in this bright sunshine of admiration and loved every second of it.

My opponent was Laura Lou Jahn, a fine player, the national junior indoor champion, but I had beaten her three times in Los Angeles, and here I was the defending champion. The year before I had trounced Anita Kanter, who in turn had eliminated Laura Lou. But this was the day Laura Lou's game caught fire. My confidence wilted, my hate grew, fear mounted, but my game would not come to a peak. I lost in three sets. Perhaps I was over-confident, lacked my usual deadly concentration, because Laura Lou, the next day, was beaten in straight sets by Patsy Zellmer, whom I had beaten countless times.

Defeat was bitter, crushing and beyond endurance. I felt utterly alone, unwanted, unliked. The crowd changed swiftly in my mind to a strange sea of unfriendly faces. Now, Laura Lou was the centre of attraction, I was shunted aside, the photographers moved in on her, and she was surrounded by admiring well-wishers.

'They hate me . . . I lost . . . but had I won, they would have liked me . . . they would have been my friends.' Such were my imaginings. I can remember vividly my feelings and thoughts at that time. It was then I was seized with the incontrovertible conviction that I must win to be liked, that only triumph would bring friends.

Eleanor Tennant contributed to my hate complex, but there was fertile soil for the seed. She believed one should not make friends with opponents, one should remain aloof. I translated this into hating my foes. Miss Tennant, I am positive, had no idea a seed of hatred would flower in my breast with such a dark bloom. Her purpose was to key my determination, force

2—FD

me to keep pressure on my opponents all the time. When she reads this, it will be the first time she will get a completely clear and penetrating picture of the champion she made.

It is not a pretty picture; the truth seldom is. I was on a collision bearing; a crack-up lay ahead as I sailed the waters of hate and fear towards a single, sure destination : a nervous breakdown.

No one, I am sure, would have believed any of this had some divining journalist put it on paper. I was popular at Cathedral High School, once president of my class, and I liked my schoolmates. They, of course, were not foes on the tennis battleground. Away from tennis, I was eager for fun, anxious to see every sight that came my way.

If my mother did not know her daughter, it was not her fault. I sought neither her counsel nor her solace. It was during this period I formed two strong friendships, both deep and lasting, both providing a safe harbour for a troubled child. Sister Adrian, the Mother Superior at Cathedral High School, knew nothing of tennis, but she did know girls, and she knew, too, that tennis was always in my heart and mind. Under less wise guidance, I could have become a girl apart in my classroom; the other students might have envied my mounting fame, become jealous of my numerous trips during schooltime. Thanks to Sister Adrian, the other girls rooted for me to win. She likewise insisted I make up every bit of work I missed. Sister Adrian carried a mental set of callipers, measured me constantly, and without her my hats might have needed alteration.

It has been my lasting regret that I did not study harder in school. Only my photographic memory enabled me to get through school early. I was an expert 'crammer,' not a dedicated scholar. There was no class in which I did not think of tennis, how I might improve my game.

The second wonderful friendship of my schooldays was with the Most Rev. Charles F. Buddy, Bishop of San Diego. This book, I fear, will come as a shock to him. He considered me an excellent example of what a young Christian girl should be, and I could not bring myself to the point where I could tell him of the hate and fear that possessed me. Of course, I was wrong. My life would have been different had I opened my heart to this churchman whose life has been a great and living example of goodness, kindness and understanding.

Despite my secretiveness, I think he sensed an inner turmoil, because he told me to come to him as I would my own father, and even though there were hundreds of demands upon his time he was always able to see me. I remember he once told me : 'Maureen, you have your own faults. Some faults in human beings are more serious than others, but each one of us is God's own creature.' He paused and smiled. 'You were endowed with a talent from the Almighty. Put it to good use. Set an example for those who follow in your footsteps. When the going becomes difficult, say a prayer and ask for Divine guidance.'

I believed whole-heartedly what this kindly man told me, and there is no capital in the tennis world where I have not prayed on the eve of a big match. But even my faith in God took a strange twist and became interwoven with my fears of losing. Because my tennis was a gift of God, losing a tournament became a rebuke from the Almighty, whom, in some manner, I had offended. Then it became time to examine not only my strokes but my conscience as well.

In this curious cauldron of my personality there was a fair dash of superstition. I had two good-luck charms and I wore them constantly after my first match against Ann Bissell. My uncle, Clarence Schwab, brought me a ring from China, and my mother had given me a heart-shaped bracelet locket. The ring had two dragons guarding a ball; to me it was a tennis ball, and they were guarding my career. Not only did I believe devoutly in the magic powers of my charms, but I also sought 'signs' in my matches, omens of good fortune. When I won the first point in my second match with Ann Bissell because the ball hit the net and trickled over for a certain point, that was a 'sign,' and it spurred me. Now, perhaps, you can understand more fully why the cry of the U.S. Air Force boy at Wimbledon struck me so deeply.

Once, in a burst of girlish confidence, I explained the magic of my good-luck charms to a priest at Cathedral High School, after we had played a match. He politely ridiculed them. I became furious. No matter how intelligently he explained things, my heart told me here was my luck. His manner became more serious as he sensed the depth of my feeling. This could have been an impasse. However, he was determined I should have no pagan gods, so he solved this dilemma in dogma by having my charms blessed !

Strangely enough, arrayed with my faith, good-luck charms and hate and fear, I had no feeling of supreme confidence, not even when I was at the pinnacle of my game. I thought at times I was good; I had the knowledge my strokes were as perfect as I could make them, that I was in such superb physical condition I could run to the moon. Still, with all this, I could endow an opponent, even a first-round foe, with superhuman ability, building her game sky-high in my mind. This, I would tell myself, would be the moment when her game would blaze and I would be beaten. Undoubtedly I attacked my weaker opponents on the court more ferociously than any other girl in the history of tennis. I 'carried' no one and this lack of confidence was the reason.

Much of this has been difficult to tell, and for my friends I know it will be difficult to believe, yet for me there could be a deep and lasting repayment. If anyone who might have started on the same path I took reads this, and then turns sharply aside, I will have a shining reward for rekindling the anguish I knew.

No fame, no approach to tennis immortality can be worth the great price I almost paid.

CHAPTER FIVE

MY RISE TO TENNIS STARDOM included two campaigns for the United States junior title at Philadelphia and my first invasions of Forest Hills. I likewise acquired a 'tennis philosophy,' which was to last throughout my career. So, to speed things up, let's telescope time a bit and go to the lovely Philadelphia Cricket Club for the finals of the juniors.

Across the court stood Laura Lou Jahn, making her fifth appearance, the runner-up the last two years, and picked by many as the most dazzling young star in tennis. A beautiful sixteen-year-old—two years older than I—Laura Lou closely resembled Lana Turner, a reigning movie queen. I hated her. She had beaten me at Coronado and I could still taste the bitterness of that defeat.

Laura Lou served. I broke her service and I beat her in straight sets, taking exactly forty-two minutes to dispose of a much more seasoned player than I. She never had a chance. I had played this match a hundred times in my mind, and, although Teach Tennant had planned no special strategy, I took the court with total concentration and a flaming resolve, which I am sure Laura Lou did not possess to the same degree.

At fourteen I became the youngest winner in the history of the junior nationals. I defended my title against Laura Lou the next year and again I beat her. In all modesty, I do not believe Laura Lou could ever have beaten me, not after her Coronado triumph. That rankled for years.

Winning the junior doubles crown, first with Lee Van Keuren of Los Angeles, and the following year with my regular partner, Patsy Zellmer, came, in both cases, as an anti-climax. This was a growing weakness in my tennis, a tendency to 'let down' after a big occasion, and it's a common fault in big-time tennis.

31

I remember clearly my doubles win with Patsy because it was a 'do or die' effort, with Patsy achieving the major share of the doing and dying. I had beaten Laura Lou, so what else was there to win? For Patsy, it was different. This was the greatest match in the world and she was determined at all costs to win it, even if it meant carrying me on her shoulders. She forced the attack, drove me every moment. 'Come on, Maureen . . . we can beat them! . . . We've got to!' I can hear her now as she played like a demon, encouraging me to rise to the occasion. Our opponents, Elaine Lewicki and Bonnie McKay, a good team, fell before Patsy's fury. I remember one sizzling forehand drive Patsy made, the ball shooting down the middle of the court and catching our opponents flatfooted. The trophy should have been awarded to Patsy. She alone deserved it.

On this trip Betty Ravenscroft Struthers, an excellent senior player, was my chaperone, and here I should like to tell you a bit about her. A San Diego girl, she played against me in the days when I could give her absolutely no competition, yet she encouraged me and went out of her way to play me. Came the day when I could beat her, and she promptly refused to play me again. 'Now, Maureen,' she said with a firm smile, 'you need tougher competition than I can give, and you should play against better girls.' Betty was completely unselfish.

One of the things which struck me about this perfectly run tournament at the Philadelphia Cricket Club was the excellent officiating. Some of the players, gifted with sharp eyes and keen reflexes, assisted the regular officials. Most of all, I recall one elderly official, who to my youthful eyes seemed to be nearly a hundred, and I can still hear him say 'OUT!' in a reedy voice that hit high C. There was nothing, however, the matter with his eyesight.

Now I would go to Forest Hills! This was in the master plan of Harper Ink, who, with the Southern California Tennis Association, sponsored my trip. Here I would play against the finest women players in the world—truly an impressive battle list— and here I was certain I would find the epitome of championship tennis. Truly, this was heady wine for a fourteen-year-old.

No one, of course, expected me to win anything, as I was stepping straight into a rarefied tennis atmosphere. Eleanor Tennant had not made the trip East with me, as even her magic could not have worked in the nationals and she had considered none of the juniors to be dangerous opponents. I, of course, expected no miracles either, but if I had to be beaten I wanted to fight savagely until the last ball was hit.

I won my first match against Marjorie Norris in straight sets and the victory set me up for my second-round match against Barbara Scofield. Here I started with a furious assault, running up a 4-1 lead in the opening set. We were in the midst of a long rally when Barbara hit a ball to my backhand corner. It was clearly out. Not by inches, but by at least a foot and a half. Barbara and I stopped play. We both knew the ball was out, but the linesman had made no ruling. I looked at him and he signalled the ball good with the flat of his hand. There was a quick roar of displeasure from the crowd. I saw red and blew up. I had been robbed! Only an idiot or a blind man could have made such a stupid call. And this at Forest Hills, where I thought the world's greatest officials presided. This was the second time in my career I had blown up and I made a beautifully thorough job of it, losing in straight sets.

'With a little more concentration, Miss Connolly might have won this match.' I quote now from *American Lawn Tennis*. I do not agree with the writer, as Barbara was a better player than I, and regardless of this incident I believe she would have won, although the match might have gone three sets. He was right, however, about my lack of concentration. I had concentration, but it was focused only on a bad call and what I considered to have been 'The Great Daylight Tennis Robbery.'

Someone, I think, once wrote about great decisions being made in a bathtub, but for me a 'tennis philosophy' came under a hot shower after that match. The warm water finally soothed me, anger dissolved, reason took hold and I held a two-way conversation with myself, the cascading water muffling the sound of my voice. I knew, unless I curbed my anger, no matter how righteous, I had absolutely no tennis future. I reasoned that by the mathematics of chance I would receive good and bad calls, but they would cancel out, strike a balance. I knew I must make myself believe that no matter how glaringly bad a call against me might be, my opponents would be subject to a similar fate. I felt at that moment my whole tennis future depended solely upon my accepting this theory with no reservations whatsoever. I did. Never again, as long as I played, did I kick at a bad call or even permit myself to think about the officiating. That was the reason Eleanor Tennant once was quoted as saying I was 'the best sportsman in tennis.'

In retrospect, any sound philosophy from a fourteen-year-old sounds highly improbable, but I think you will agree that I was no ordinary little girl, and tennis was not just a game. It was my very life. I have thought of that philosophical shower many times, and the incident came back to me vividly at Wimbledon that year when Vic Seixas blew up, causing one of the London newspapers to exclaim : 'Good gracious, Mr. Seixas !'

Following Forest Hills, I returned to California, where the famous Pacific Southwest Championships are next on the big-time American schedule. It was here I met Shirley Fry for the first time, and she was one of the great players while I was unseeded. Before I take you into that match, I should like to tell you of a wonderful experience I had. The Helms Athletic Foundation, a famous California organization devoted to amateur sports, voted me the Southern California Athlete of the Month for becoming the youngest girl in history to win the national juniors. There was a centre-court presentation at the Los Angeles Tennis Club and a huge birthday cake was wheeled out, because this was September 17th and I was fifteen years old.

Now, my match against Shirley Fry. I did not use my secret weapons of hate and fear because I was a realist and wasted no ammunition on lost causes. Shirley was an international star and I knew I did not belong on the same court with her. Perhaps she loafed, because I took the first set from her before she turned

on the pressure and steam-rollered me, taking the next two sets
6-2, 6-2. Until that match, I had never entertained the hope
of beating her, but now the thought came to me that surely I
could beat her in the future.

I have saved a description of Forest Hills because I wanted
to wait until my second trip there to tell you about it. The
important matches—at least, the ones the officials think will be
the most interesting—are played on the stadium courts. The
centre court is reserved for the semi-finals and finals, but it is a
high honour to play on either of the two courts which flank it.
There are about twenty grass courts on the grounds outside the
stadium, and that's where I had played my previous matches.
This time I managed to get inside.

I was fifteen years old and had successfully defended my
junior title before coming to the nationals. I reached the third
round only to meet the girl I considered to be the greatest
player in the world—Doris Hart. She was my idol, the epitome
of a champion, the personification of charm and friendliness, and
I worshipped her. I had watched her play many times with
wondrous eyes, hoping there would be a far-away day when I
might approach her prowess. It would have been inconceivable
then for me to have hated Doris. Our tennis was still worlds
apart.

I remember once we were sitting in the players' section and
the girls wanted some ice cream. 'You are the youngest, junior,
you run and get it,' Doris told me. I would have sprinted around
the block, gladly.

The players' main entrance to the stadium courts is under a
striped marquee and there are four brick steps leading to the
courts. Like Wimbledon, there is a plaque for the players, but
with a different motto: 'It Matters Not Whether You Win or
Lose, but How You Play the Game.' I took one glance and
differed sharply.

It is customary for the players to meet on the brick steps,
then wait for the match to be announced. Doris joined me, took
one look at my jittery stance, my taut expression, and did a rare

and wonderful thing. She tried her best to put me at ease. Her smile was warm, friendly, sincere and she wanted to know how I felt. 'A little scared,' I managed to reply in the understatement of the year. She told me she felt exactly the same way (a sweet white lie), and then she gave me this advice : 'Forget about the stadium and the crowd and just concentrate on playing your best game. Remember, the crowd will be with you all the way.' (I did not know then that the crowd always roots for the underdog.)

We stood there, and there were several beats of silence before a gong-like sound rang over the public address system—the signal for another match. My heart skipped a few beats. Then the announcer introduced Doris, giving the long and impressive list of her tournament victories. Now it was my turn. 'Miss Maureen Connolly, the United States Junior National champion,' he said, and stopped. I had no other titles. There was a pause, then he added, perhaps to bolster me : 'And a promising little player.' ('A frightened little girl' would have been more accurate.)

Those four brick steps to the courts became like the thirteen steps to the gallows for me, and I was certain this would be a mid-afternoon execution, but despite my stage fright I played well. Doris threw me an occasional smile across the court, and with this encouragement I relaxed a bit. I was proud of getting two games off her in the first set, as I expected to lose love and love.

In the second set, I caught fire, my game blazed and soared, my drives hit the lines, and I was way over my head. I shot into a 4-3 lead. As we changed courts and I towelled off, the sudden, shocking realization hit me : 'My heavens, I am leading Doris. This can't be possible !' My concentration broke completely. The situation now appeared utterly fantastic. How could I, an unknown, possibly be in front of this great player? I did not stay in front long. Doris turned on the pressure, began forcing me, and ran off the set 6-4.

But even in defeat I felt wonderful. I had expected to have

been blasted off the court, but I hadn't been. I had played well, the crowd had cheered for me, even entertained the thought I might fashion a miraculous upset. A feeling of pure exhilaration rose in me.

Doris and I walked off the court together, or perhaps I floated off, the cheers of the crowd still in my ears. Doris smiled at me out of her big, beautiful brown eyes, the pressure of her hand on my arm was firm and friendly.

'Maureen,' she said, 'you certainly have improved since I saw you play last June. You have a fine future.' The queen had spoken, my heart beat faster, and Doris was still my idol, but the pedestal was higher.

I took one last look at the huge crowd, my eyes went up to the impressive eagles, executed in cement, which ring the top of the horseshoe-shaped stadium. Then I looked back at the crowd, and I remember the moment clearly. This setting no longer held terror for me, and I thought to myself :

'You will see a lot more of me in the future !'

CHAPTER SIX

FOREST HILLS now became my bright shining goal, and victory in the centre court my dream, but along this high road lay hundreds of hours of practice, dozens of tournaments. But more than anything else, my torrid matches against Nancy Chaffee helped pave the way, and had it not been for Nancy, a great player and a dear friend, I should not have become the youngest women's champion in United States tennis history. She gave my game a polish it lacked. Beating her gave me a new confidence.

Nancy is a beautiful girl, vivacious, full of fun, and she has large, luminous green eyes, which, combined with a smooth tan, make her really striking. She is six years older than I, and still one of America's great players.

I was sixteen years old when I first played Nancy, and although I had twice been to Forest Hills I did not yet entertain any serious hopes of beating the top senior women. The juniors, of course, held no terrors for me, but the seniors . . . that was something else again. It may have been that my first tour, when I was thirteen, gave me a bit of an inferiority complex, because each time I had stepped out of my division Beverly Baker had blasted me off the court.

Nancy was the 'big name' and the No. 1 seed at the Palm Springs tournament. She was seeded among the top five nationally, she held a tournament triumph over Louise Brough, the world's champion, and now at this fashionable California desert resort she was expected to romp through the opposition.

For me this tournament offered great opportunity, and I had worked tirelessly to bring my game to a peak for it. Hate and fear powered me as I cut down my early-round foes to reach the finals and a chance to play Nancy. Like Doris Hart, I held

Nancy in high admiration, although my concentration was absolute as I took the court, my determination to win flaming high. I took the first set 6-3. I was leading in the second set 4-1 when Nancy defaulted.

The tournament was mine, but this was no victory at all. I wanted nothing by default. Furthermore, Nancy was nowhere near the top of her game. She was ill with influenza, running a fever, and shouldn't have been on the court. 'Maureen,' she said to me, 'I just can't go on. . . . I'll have to default, and I'm terribly sorry.' This stunned me. My total concentration had been on the match, on winning. I mumbled something in return and walked off the court, forlorn and crushed, even though this was my biggest triumph to date.

Bill Tilden, whom I considered to have been the world's greatest player, was standing on the sidelines. 'Congratulations, Mo !' he sang out.

'For what?' I asked dejectedly.

'You won the match,' he said quietly.

'I didn't win it, really. Nancy had to default.'

'Listen, Maureen,' Bill said seriously. 'Don't ever forget this will go down in the record books as a win.' He paused, and added softly : 'There will come a time when you'll wish your opponent would default.' (How prophetic that was !)

'I'd rather lose than win by default,' I shot back.

He smiled indulgently, shook his head, shrugged his shoulders, and told me : 'Run along and take your shower.'

Nancy was in the dressing-room and she saw at once how disappointed I was and did her best to cheer me up. She knew, too, how much I liked her. One of my most thrilling girlish moments had been when I had asked Nancy for her autograph and she had written, 'To Maureen—the 1955 World's Champion,' and that was long before many people had taken me or my tennis seriously.

'There will be other tournaments,' Nancy said gently, 'and we both will be in them.' (Here was a quick blueprint of the future.)

Nancy had a splendid offer at this time to turn professional, but after her default to me at Palm Springs the promoter stipulated she should not play me again. My win, of course, could have been written off as a fluke, but Nancy disregarded both the offer and the advice. She entered a number of small tournaments I was in, and the only reason she included these in her itinerary was to give me a chance to play her.

I won every match against Nancy, improving with each one, gaining confidence from this hard, close competition. Our matches were all three-setters, exceptionally close, with only a point or two separating us. Nancy had a better serve than I, the best forehand in women's tennis, but to offset this I had the better backhand and I was fleeter of foot. The essential difference between us, I think, was my tremendous competitive spirit and total concentration. Nancy would have an occasional lapse in concentration.

One match comes back vividly. Nancy and I were in the finals at Ojai, California, and in the gallery was the incomparable Jack Kramer. Nancy and I, as always, split sets, but she was off to a blazing start in the final set, running up a 4-1 lead. Then she had a slight lapse. This is difficult for me to explain, hard for the casual spectator to observe, but there can come a moment when some of the sting goes out of your opponent's game, the bouncy walk is lacking, the confident stance for a return of service is missing. The previous fight and fire have diminished, although the degree may be slight. It happened then. I knew, despite the fact Nancy had run me ragged, the tide was at ebb and I could turn it. Such a situation has always been a secret signal for me to pour every ounce of fuel into my game, sometimes drawing upon a reserve I was not quite certain was there.

I fought back furiously, brought the match even, then we won our services until I finally broke through, taking the set, 10-8. 'I really thought I had you that time, Maureen,' Nancy told me. And from Jack Kramer I received this thrilling compliment: 'That was a great comeback. You really are a little fighter, Maureen.'

Nancy, who now is Mrs. Ralph Kiner, America's former baseball home-run king, lives in San Diego, where Ralph is general manager of the baseball team. We occasionally rehash some of our matches, and they have remained just as bright in memory for her as they have for me. Perhaps you would like a bit of Nancy off the cuff :

'If I hadn't been in love with Kiner,' she told me, 'you would have broken my heart. I was playing my best tennis, love had given me a lift, but I couldn't beat you and I wanted to so much. I wanted Ralph to be proud of me, I wanted to be just as good a tennis player as he was a ball player. [Kiner led the major-league hitters for seven straight years.] Losing to you so steadily was a terribly disappointing experience. Towards the end, I think I developed a defeatist attitude. But you must have known, Maureen, you could always beat me.'

I didn't, however, know I could always beat Nancy, and if this statement needs a bit of shoring up I can give you somewhat graphic documentation. The tournament in question was at Pebble Beach, California, and my chaperones were William Scripps Kellogg (Bill to a legion of tennis friends) and his charming wife, Alice. Kellogg is trustee and managing director of the famed La Jolla Beach and Tennis Club and an internationally known tennis figure. He is a member of the executive committee of the United States Lawn Tennis Association; he represented the United States at Wimbledon and France in 1956; he also is vice-president of the Southern California Tennis Association, and has a few other titles and membership on important committees.

We were staying at the Pebble Beach Lodge, and this was the day of the finals in which I was to play Nancy again. We had attended church services at the Carmel Mission. Later, at breakfast, I made a horrible discovery. I had lost my heart-shaped bracelet locket! I began crying. I told Mr. Kellogg I simply could not play Nancy in the finals that morning without my bracelet. I would surely lose! Kellogg looked at me for a moment in stunned silence as my sobs continued. His background of success, however, had not been founded upon inaction.

A search! This was no ordinary search, but an investigation in the classic French detective tradition. Kellogg had my room gone over inch by inch, then, meeting failure, he worked backwards retracing our steps until he found the bracelet! It was lying by the kerb in front of the Carmel Mission, but it apparently had been run over by a car; it was broken and I could not wear it. To compound the dilemma, no jewellery stores were open on Sunday. Kellogg stopped at a garage, but here the mechanic did not have fine enough wire to repair it. Then Kellogg had a frustrating telephonic experience with the town's three jewellers, none of whom was willing to open up shop for a fast repair job. One jeweller complained he had stayed up all night making out Government forms, that he was so disgusted with the political party then in power that he was seriously considering quitting business.

Kellogg then tried another garage, found some fine wire and promptly performed the only jewellery repair job in his life! No craftsman could have done better. (Later, Rube Samuelsen, sports editor of the *Pasadena Star-News*, got an inkling of this incident, went to Kellogg and asked him to elaborate. Kellogg, however, had become so certain my tennis future was interlaced with the black magic of good-luck charms that he persuaded Samuelsen not to use the story. Kellogg thought there would be a chance someone might steal the locket, and there would go my tennis career.)

I took the court against Nancy, my bracelet and ring protecting me, and I beat her in three long, hard sets. Could I have won without the bracelet? The simple truth is: had not Mr. Kellogg found and repaired the bracelet I would have defaulted to Nancy, and no tournament committee could have changed my decision.

As a footnote to my tennis warfare with Nancy, a brief

description by Nelson Fisher of the *San Diego Union* might interest you :

'These matches were among the most thrilling in the history of tennis. Maureen and Nancy, both extremely hard-hitting players, were masters of the backcourt. The style of each complemented the other. Certainly, these combined styles were unique in women's tennis, and, for the spectator, the big thrill came because they were so evenly matched.'

La Jolla Beach and Tennis Club's annual Invitational Tournament triggers the American season each spring, and, since its inception in 1942, many winners have gone on to national championships and the world's title at Wimbledon. This year, when I was sixteen, I was entered in this event. Although some of the more seasoned stars regarded no spring event as important, and for that matter considered nothing in American tennis really vital save Forest Hills, I did not then share their view.

To me, the Beach Club Invitational was tremendously important. I had toiled furiously to be ready for it, practised night and day.

Because of defaults, I played only one match to reach the finals, and this was against Barbara Kimbrell, whom I defeated 6-2, 6-1. I expected to play Pat Todd in the finals as she was top-seeded, and, of course, a great star. However, Mrs. Mary Arnold Prentiss, National Public Parks champion, vanquished Miss Todd 6-2, 4-6, 6-4.

With Eleanor Tennant on the sidelines, I faced Mrs. Prentiss, sure my game was right, confident my serve, which Teach had been working on, would click. Both my ground strokes and my serve worked perfectly. The weather was windy, but I was not. I hit a pattern of hard cross-court forehands and backhands. Mrs. Prentiss's serve was not effective, and often I had a set-up shot for a sure placement. I beat her 6-3, 6-4, to capture the women's crown.

Ahead lay Forest Hills !

CHAPTER SEVEN

MY TRIUMPH AT FOREST HILLS, when I became the youngest tennis champion in the history of the United States, was a strange drama—a play within a play, seen by thousands, understood by none—told now for the first time. It was a story that circled the globe, yet of all who wrote about it not a single one knew the real reasons for victory, the true motivation, which shot me to the top.

I was the girl with the Golden Racket that glorious summer when I was sixteen, and the drama began with the tournament at the Merion Cricket Club in Philadelphia, which pops the cork on the Eastern tennis season. The beginning was especially wonderful for me because I was the house guest of Mr. and Mrs. William Clothier at their Valley Forge home near Merion. They are devotees of the fox-hunt, maintain their own pack, and have some wonderful hunters, so I had a chance to ride and I loved every moment of it.

I would go against a tough tennis field, but now I was no longer a timid junior, but a star on the rise. Under my belt were the series of victories over Nancy Chaffee and a triumph over Louise Brough. I watched the other girls with a cold, critical eye. Beverly Baker stood out in my draw and I thought she would be my most formidable foe. Eleanor Tennant had remained in La Jolla, staying with her sister, Gwen, who was dying. My chaperone was Sophie Fisher, a dear friend and wife of Nelson Fisher, tennis writer for the *San Diego Union*.

My early-round matches went smoothly as I dynamited my way towards Beverly and the semi-finals. Every chance I had I watched her. Under ordinary circumstances, Beverly would have loomed as an insurmountable hurdle. She had crushed me so many times before, but now I was more confident, and as I

44

watched her win her early-round matches I thought she looked tired and drawn as if she might have left her best tennis at Wimbledon, where she had fallen before Doris Hart. She wasn't hitting as well as I knew she could. I kept telling myself this was the time when I would have a real chance against her. Ordinarily, the huge backlog of Beverly's victories over me would have acted as a psychological stumbling-block. But not now!

I charged into battle against Beverly, determined to beat her, ready to even old scores, certain the hour of revenge had come. I never eased the savage pressure, forcing her every inch of the way. I defeated her in straight sets 6-4, 6-3, sweeping five of the last six games with a loss of eight points. This was my first triumph over Beverly and it lifted me up for the finals.

There I ran into a Tartar—Betty Rosenquest—who had blasted Pat Todd of La Jolla, the U.S. hard court champion, off the court 6-4, 6-0. I had never played Betty, and never had I gone against such a baffling array of chops and slices in my life. I caught her at a peak; on a day, to quote one tennis writer, when she was playing far over her head. I can remember the match vividly and still feel the exhaustion which gripped me. My surging attack brought me the first set, 7-5. Then Betty, a much more seasoned campaigner that I, centred her offence on my weak short game, exploiting it to the hilt, taking the set 6-4. I later discovered Betty is not an exceptionally steady player, but she was rock-like this day. I was on the edge of defeat several times in the third set, but I finally won it 7-5, but only my hate, power and speed carried me through this gruelling hour and thirty-five minutes. Betty, by the way, gave me a tennis education that day, and what I learned about her particular type of game I was to use against her with advantage later.

Now let's quicken the tempo. My tennis went sour at the next tournament at the Maidstone Club at East Hampton, Long Island. Sophie Fisher became alarmed and telephoned her husband, in San Diego, who had helped me so much with my career. Nelson acted quickly, bought an airplane ticket and took it to Eleanor Tennant at her La Jolla home, where he painted a dark picture of my tennis. By this time Eleanor's sister, Gwen, was beyond medical help. Previously, Gwen, who knew she was dying, had implored Eleanor to go on this Eastern tour with me, but Teach, who loved her sister dearly and had taken care of her for years, hated to leave her. But now Eleanor knew the long vigil was almost at an end. She took the plane East.

I fell before Pat Todd in the semi-finals at the Maidstone Club tournament in a three-setter. She beat me 3-6, 6-3, 7-5. I had her match point, 40-0 in the third set, but I couldn't put over a victory as 'Toddy' fought back, playing truly magnificent tennis.

My troubles continued at South Orange, New Jersey, where the Eastern Lawn Tennis Championships are held. Here I injured my ankle and foot when I tripped over a linesman's chair. Fortunately, it was not too serious, but I incurred the wrath of Miss Tennant, when, instead of resting my ankle, I slipped out to a dance and took a fling at doing the Charleston. Again, Pat Todd became my Nemesis, eliminating me 3-6, 6-4, 6-2.

I played next at the Essex tournament at Manchester, Massachusetts, and here I met Beverly Baker, but this time I vanquished her again. In the semi-finals I faced my idol, Doris Hart. Against her, of course, I knew I had absolutely no chance. However, I did manage to get set point before losing the first set 10-8. Doris took the second set easily, 6-2. I thought I had done awfully well against her, but, as I was to learn later, Teach thought something entirely different.

During the national doubles at the Longwood Cricket Club, where I failed to distinguish myself on the courts, we were staying at the home of Mrs. Hazel Wightman, founder of the Wightman Cup matches. She lives at Chestnut Hill, a fashionable suburb of Boston, and her home is only a block and a half from the Cricket Club. It was there I received an invitation from Mrs. Richard (Midge) Buck to play on the United States Wightman Cup team, which she captained.

This posed a problem itinerary that year. My mother wanted me to defend my United States Junior title at Philadelphia and she was opposed to my going against the top senior women, believing I was not yet ready. Teach had taken a violently opposite view. To her, the Juniors means less than nothing. She thought I would breeze through the field, reap a lot of publicity and the harvest would be a swelled head. No series of easy matches, she reasoned, could possibly get me ready for the big ones ahead. I was thrilled with Midge Buck's invitation and wanted to play, but it meant leaving my Junior title undefended, since the Wightman Cup and Junior Championship were both held at the same time, and also disappointing my doubles partner, Patsy Zellmer. Mrs. Wightman thought I had many years ahead of me to play in the Cup matches and she advocated the Juniors. I spent a miserable evening of indecision, then I telephoned to Patsy in Philadelphia; she urged me to play in the Wightman Cup. That settled it, and now I was ready for this inspiring event at the Longwood Cricket Club.

Just recently, Eleanor Tennant revealed she played a backstage role in my selection for the United States team. There was a bit of polite deprecation when my name was mentioned; there were other girls seeded higher who deserved the honour more. Then Teach announced I would become the United States champion that year, and when I did she would go to the Press and reveal that the best woman player in America had been forced to sit on the sidelines. Eleanor is a dynamic and forceful woman, highly convincing, and if she told anyone flatly I would become the champion I know the statement came with ringing authority.

The Wightman Cup is like nothing else in tennis, and for the women it's the closest thing to the Davis Cup, although competition has always been limited to England and the United States. (Here, I should like to make a plea for widening the scope of these matches to include a number of other tennis-playing nations. Certainly it would strengthen women's tennis throughout the world, setting a high inspirational goal.)

Wearing the United States team insignia, hearing the American and English national anthems played, is an experience that gives one a soaring sensation. In the play, it isn't 'Point, Connolly,' but 'Point, United States' or 'Point, England.' It is as if the fate of one's country were at stake—a do-or-die thing —and there can be no retreat.

I played only one match and this against Kay Tuckey, an exceptionally fine player. I took the court supercharged with patriotism, ready to race my legs off for a return. I won the first set 6-1, but I was certain Kay would rise up and crush me the next two sets, and as we changed courts this fear almost choked me.

'Midge, Midge, what'll I do now?' I implored. I wanted a quick and magic formula for victory. Midge smiled at me from her captain's chair on the court and replied calmly : 'Maureen, you are doing fine. Just keep on doing whatever you want to do.' Midge's face was serene, reflecting complete confidence.

It is hardly likely Kay Tuckey thought the British Empire would crumble if she lost, but I was certain the weight of all America rested squarely on my young shoulders. I won the second set 6-3, and towards the end of it, when I knew I had a sure win, I felt for the first time in my life an equality with the best American girls, an inner feeling that I might be as good as they.

Our team won the Wightman Cup that year, and Teach, who may have been prejudiced, said I played better tennis than any girl on the United States team. I know my play reached heights which would normally have been beyond me. I watched the other matches critically, sure I could beat a few of the stars who I previously thought twinkled too brightly for me.

It was about this time a stray mosquito nipped me on the leg; infection set in and the leg became swollen. Teach insisted I see a doctor, but I didn't think it was serious. We had a somewhat violent argument before I submitted to medical care. Another quarrel involved a dinner party I attended, and my getting to bed late instead of retiring at an early hour as Teach had ordered. Disagreements were becoming the pattern of our relationship.

Forest Hills! Here would be the burial of hope or the climax of desire, and it looked, even before the tournament began, as if hope should be abandoned. I was practising on an outer court with Charley Hare when I stepped on a ball and hurt my ankle again. More hot packs! But this time I did no dancing. Well, the tournament got under way, but my tennis dazzled no one in the early rounds. I did, however, reach the semi-finals.

Here I would meet the real champion, Doris Hart, the Wimbledon winner, the one girl in tennis whom I worshipped, who could do no wrong, and whom I wanted to emulate as a person and a player more than anyone else in the world. And it was here Eleanor Tennant, certain I would be beaten, gambled boldly on devious strategy. Eleanor told Sophie Fisher that Doris, under the surface of her charm, disliked me intensely and had said: 'Maureen is a spoiled brat. . . . I'm gunning for her . . . and I'm going to give her a tennis lesson.' This, of course, was a complete fabrication, and Sophie, who knew Doris, did not believe it. But she understood the motivation and knew Eleanor counted on her to tell me. For Sophie it was an extremely difficult position and hers was a hard decision to make. But she felt as Teach did that I could not beat Doris unless my hero-worship was broken. So, she told me.

No idol fell faster or with a more shattering crash than Doris Hart. I was shocked, stunned, then I saw blinding red. I phoned Teach immediately, but one galvanizing gambit was not enough for Miss Tennant. She jolted me further by saying she was too busy to see me that evening, she couldn't care less about my prospects. She topped that off by telling me she was trying to get a reservation for a plane to Boston in the morning. I spent a storm-tossed night, but I phoned Eleanor the next morning and she agreed to see me. (The Boston trip, of course, had been as fictional as Doris's remarks.)

I hurried to see Teach, asked her if she would go with me to see Doris Hart and straighten things out. She flatly refused.

'Do you want Doris as a friend?' she asked.

'Yes, I do.'

'Do you want her respect?'

'Yes.'

'There is only one way to get it. Go out and beat her this afternoon. If you do that, if you play tennis, I will stay here and you can win the title.'

And so that afternoon on the centre court at Forest Hills I faced Doris Hart. I never hated anyone more in my life! I turned on her like a tiger, but despite my fury—I tried to knock the cover off the ball—I managed to lose the first four games.

Teach sat calmly in the stands watching the match. A friend beside her remarked: 'Well, it is no disgrace for Maureen to lose to such a seasoned player.' Teach turned and announced with finality: 'Connolly will win!' Miss Tennant claims she gets a ticking sensation in the solar plexus when one of her champions is playing well. This strange beat was steady now.

On the courts a drizzle began to fall. I charged wildly for everything, totally oblivious of the footing, consumed with hate and fiery determination. I won six straight games and the set! I played some of the greatest tennis of my career. I shot for the lines, made impossible returns, applied crushing pressure, forced my foe every second. No sane player would have taken the reckless gambles I did. The sting went out of Doris's game when the drizzle started. I stood ready to continue the match in a downpour, but the officials postponed it until the next day.

My hate for Doris did not flag the next afternoon. I wanted to blast her off the court in a love set. I surged into a 5-1 lead. The crowd leaned forward, certain a big upset was near. Then miraculously, as often happens in championship tennis, Doris suddenly became invincible, played brilliantly, forced a withering attack, achieved perfect placements. She pulled up to 4-5.

Then came the 'pressure game' of all time for me. I was only a few points from victory; Doris only a few points from squaring the match. If she could do this, reach such a plateau, after having been in an almost impossible position, the psychology of the situation would become for her a miraculous weapon.

We played down the middle, hitting hard, but steering the safe course as the game seesawed. Then it became her advantage, my serve; caution clutched me and I gave her a forehand set-up. For Doris, tension had built sky-high. She 'choked,' her racket wavered, she misjudged the set-up and the ball rolled to net and with it went Doris's hopes. I knew I had her! I slammed over a hard placement, catching her unexpectedly off balance to win advantage. Then she netted a high backhand volley. I won the match!

Fury still gripped me as I left the courts and joined Teach and Sophie under the marquee. 'Well, I guess I showed her if I was a spoiled brat!' I told them. Mervyn Rose, the Australian star, was standing near by. Much later he told me: 'Maureen, I have never seen an expression like yours on anyone's face.'

For me, Forest Hills was over, the tournament won, the biggest game of all lay dead in my trophy bag. The let-down was tremendous. I had beaten the Wimbledon champion, the one girl I thought to be the greatest in the world. Shirley Fry, whom I would meet the next day in the finals, had lost many tournaments to Doris, but she could be dangerous, even invincible, if I were not at a peak.

I awoke early the morning of the finals, terribly nervous, wound up tight, edgy, jittery, and of all things I wanted a black evening dress. I had to have it now; nothing else in the world seemed important. So we drove into New York. The saleswoman listened to my request, smiled pleasantly, and said she had nothing suitable. The only black dress in my size was for an older woman. But I had to see it! The gown, slinky, strapless, tight-fitting, with a slit up the side, was strictly an 'other woman' costume. I have never worn it, but the moment I bought it the tension subsided, my obsession was satisfied, a lassitude set in.

The finals, I knew, would be hard fought. I believed I had a better chance here, and I was especially happy that Nelson Fisher had flown in from San Diego to cover the event for his newspaper. I knew my tennis had reached a peak and, after all, I felt Shirley Fry was no Doris Hart.

How wrong can one be? Eleanor Tennant had invented a device for me to beat Doris, but it boomeranged. My victory acted as a sharp spur for Shirley. She and Doris were the closest and best friends in the world, travelled together, were inseparable. Shirley could lose to Doris with grace, but to see a sixteen-year-old cut down her friend was something else again. I do not know if she took the court with hatred, but she did take it with great determination.

I played my best tennis in the first set, shooting for the lines; everything clicking perfectly, and, as I took it, 6-3, I was sure victory lay just ahead, mine for the asking.

The second set began promisingly. I broke Shirley's service, but this was the only game I won. Shirley fathomed my attack and revised her strategy, mixing her shots, accenting angles, giving me higher balls, shorter shots, exercising uncanny control. This was a rout. I went for everything. My tongue literally hung out with exhaustion.

Describing the match to a friend, Eleanor said : 'My heart went out for Maureen. Never, before or since, has Shirley played such great tennis. She was out for revenge . . . she was inspired.'

Had this match been played at Wimbledon, I think unquestionably Shirley would have won the third set, possibly at love. But at Forest Hills there is a ten-minute rest period before the third set. Teach waited for me in the dressing-room. Then she manufactured a miracle, rubbing the tiredness out of my legs, massaging my shoulders, strength flowing from her fingers, but more than anything else her compelling voice charged me. 'You will have to control your hitting,' Teach told me. 'To do that you'll have to move faster . . . and you'll have to do it . . . even if it kills you to win this set. Forget you're tired. . . . You're in the big leagues now . . . you can't submit to fatigue. Concentrate on your game . . . you must win!' I looked at Teach, my confidence rising, and said : 'I'm going to get her!'

I charged on the court with flaming resolve and absolute concentration. My fatigue vanished. With Teach in the wings I could not fail. This was war. Shirley's attack was dangerous, but it no longer baffled me to the same degree. There were bitter volleys when the ball must have gone off our rackets twenty-five times. The game score reached 4 all. I won my service, losing only one point, bringing it to 5-4. Shirley took the attack, ran the next game to 40-15. I fought back savagely, brought it to 40-30, then deuce. Twice more it went to deuce, then my advantage. Suddenly it dawned on me I was only one point away from becoming the youngest American champion in history! This realization came with crushing impact. I was petrified with fear. My arms and legs seemed to turn to stone. It took superhuman effort to return Shirley's service. The ball shot back and forth as we blasted forehands in a long rally. Then I hit a short backhand cross-court to her backhand. Shirley sizzled a spectacular backhand return down my forehand. I was flatfooted. I couldn't move. 'It's out! . . . It's out!' I prayed to myself. It was! By inches!

I was the champion! I came out of my trance, raced to the net, letting out a war-whoop on the way. I was laughing, crying, delirious, almost hysterical. Twenty-eight years ago, the great Helen Wills had won at seventeen, but now a new chapter had been written.

I was the American champion at sixteen!

CHAPTER EIGHT

'THE CENTRE COURT at Wimbledon is like a tiny postage stamp in the middle of a huge envelope. There is nothing like it in the world!' This vivid description by Tony Trabert, the American star, became my first mental impression of Wimbledon, but when I arrived there in 1952 the picture became magnified many times.

Although I was now going after the greatest title of all, this was far from a happy time in my career. Eleanor Tennant thought I was stale, that I had left my game in San Diego. I was not playing my best in the English events leading up to Wimbledon. Then, when I was practising for the Wightman Cup matches, I developed a sore shoulder due solely to my own carelessness. I was hot, perspiring, and I stood and talked in chilling weather, without even bothering to put on a sweater. Eleanor wanted me to drop out of the tournament at Queen's, but this was on my schedule and I wanted to play in it, hoping my shoulder might improve. However, during one of the matches, the pain became so intense that I defaulted and hurried away without giving an explanation. Later, Teach told the Press I defaulted because of the severe pain. Foolishly I denied this, as I did not want to use my shoulder as an alibi.

Teach sent me first to a soccer trainer, who diagnosed the shoulder as bursitis and suggested liniment. Then she took me to a chiropractor, who diagnosed my trouble as a torn muscle. This touched off another row between Teach and me. She thought my whole future would be in jeopardy, but I could not agree. My shoulder did not hurt when I hit a forehand drive or backhand, but only an overhead shot. I was certain it couldn't be a torn muscle.

My woes became page-one news in London—our hotel a day-and-night bivouac for the Press. One photographer burst into our apartment one evening demanding I pose in the bathtub nursing my shoulder. Then a story broke quoting a doctor as saying I had been given a series of novocaine injections to deaden my shoulder pain. This was an outright lie, without a tissue of truth, and the doctor was later expelled from membership of the All England Lawn Tennis Club.

There are two versions of my break with Teach, mine and hers. This is my story and I shall tell it now for the first time, as I remember it. We were having tea in the players' tea-room over the No. 1 court at Wimbledon and the current argument was about mixed doubles. I was scheduled to play with Mervyn Rose and Teach wanted me to withdraw. I refused.

The big blow fell immediately afterwards when Teach was quoted as having said she was washing her hands of me, that I was headstrong, wouldn't listen to her advice and was putting my career in jeopardy. Now, I had no chance at Wimbledon, the story went. Teach was quoted as advocating my withdrawal from the singles, while, as a matter of fact, only mixed doubles had been under discussion. Other stories asked if all this were a publicity stunt. I was stunned, bewildered, confused and almost on the verge of a nervous breakdown. Even during our quarrels, the thought of going into battle at Wimbledon without Teach had never occurred to me. My final emotion, however, was anger.

Mom had borne the telephonic brunt of the Press storm and the phone never stopped ringing. Even bookies called and wanted 'inside information.' My mother was distraught. She knew what Wimbledon meant to me, but she wasn't sure whether or not I should play. Finally, she called Perry T. Jones for help. Jones had never been to England before. In fact, he had never been outside California, but this year he and his sister, Mrs. Llewellyn Brown, had come to Wimbledon with Mr. and Mrs. William Scripps Kellogg of La Jolla. He was assisting Russell D. Kingman, chairman of the United States

Lawn Tennis Association's International Play Committee. I have always thought it a strange twist of fate that Jones should be in London for the first and only time just when I most needed his help.

Recently, Jones gave this version of his part in my troubles :

'I had read in the newspapers about Maureen's shoulder and later the diversity of opinion existing between Maureen and Miss Tennant. I recoiled from entering any argument and I remained on the sidelines until Maureen's mother telephoned me and pleaded for help. She told me I was the only one who could possibly straighten out the situation. I said I would help, but only if they would follow my advice implicitly. This was agreed. I wanted to get the best orthopaedic man in London and I enlisted the aid of Dr. J. C. Gregory (now president of the All England Lawn Tennis Club). He suggested three top men but finally a Dr. Knowland was selected. I then phoned Maureen and told her of the appointment, but, before she went, there would be an irrevocable stipulation. She would withdraw immediately if the doctor advised it. This was agreed to by both Maureen and her mother.'

Our trip to the hospital was a 'cops and robbers' chase as we tried vainly to shake off the pursuing journalists. No girl ever entered the portals of medicine with more fear or misgivings than I. I felt as though my very life hung in the balance as the doctor, a distinguished-looking man, examined my shoulder. He was thorough, painstaking, and after an eternity he finished.

'My dear,' he began softly, 'you haven't a torn muscle . . .'

I had my arms around him, kissing him with wild joy before he completed the sentence. I was certain he never encountered a more excited patient or made a diagnosis which was received with such hysterical enthusiasm.

After my emotional outburst was spent, he explained with rare kindness that I had fibrositis—a type of congestion in the shoulder muscle. He promptly made an appointment for me to see an osteopath at once. I couldn't wait! The osteopath told

me to put my arms behind my back, then he gave a quick
upward jerk and I felt a blinding, shooting pain in my shoulder.
Miraculously, in a few moments it felt better. Next, I was given
a series of machine treatments with a device which flexes one's
muscles involuntarily, thus breaking up the congestion. I continued these treatments twice a day throughout Wimbledon.

We were staying at the White House Apartments in London,
and Teach was living there, too. In order to avoid any further
Press flare-up, we maintained a sham truce with Miss Tennant.
Jones had insisted there be an absolute minimum of publicity.
I'm sure by then everyone was fed up with my troubles and I
confined my reading to the dinner menu. I do recall that the
players were a bit cool to me, and certainly the gallery was
against me.

Now I should like to give you some of the full flavour of
Wimbledon. I was a nervous seventeen-year-old when I first
met Duncan MacAulay, secretary of the All England Lawn
Tennis Club, received my credentials, tickets for meals, seats and
a player's badge. Mr. MacAulay's charm was wasted upon a
daytime sleepwalker mumbling her thanks.

Next came the dressing-room assignments. There are two
dressing-rooms at Wimbledon, geographically close, but con-
tinents apart in caste. The upper dressing-room is reserved for
former Wimbledon champions, the ranking players of the
various nations, and for members of the All England Lawn
Tennis Club. Assigned to the lower dressing-room are the
unseeded players, the unknowns. Rivalry for the upper dressing-
room is intense. I was prepared to be assigned to the lower
room. Though I was the American champion and had beaten
Doris Hart and Shirley Fry to get there, I had no confidence in
myself, and there were many people who thought my Forest
Hills win was a fluke. I thought it was lucky, and, after all,
what did a win at Forest Hills mean at this world's shrine of
tennis? This should give you an idea of the awe I felt, how
impressed I was. I floated on a cloud when I was told to go to
the upper dressing-room.

I paused in a small round hall and stood spellbound before a huge board, where, in gold letters, were the names of the former Wimbledon champions, the dates of their triumphs. Before me rose the names of the legendary Suzanne Lenglen and Helen Wills, and I thought no matter how desperately I tried I could never match their feats of court wizardry. Suddenly the gold letters struck a note of terror. The name of Louise Brough appeared three times. At the top of the list loomed Doris Hart, the 1951 winner. Both of these great American players might be my foes, if I lasted that long. Then a smothered thought arose : Would my name be next? I smiled. It seemed almost too much to hope for then. As I turned to go up the stairs, I saw a small wooden plaque above the waiting-room door. It read : 'If you can meet with triumph and disaster and treat these two impostors just the same.' I said a silent prayer, asking for triumph.

I walked upstairs, knocked timidly on the dressing-room door and it was opened by Mrs. Ward, the dressing-room mistress, a petite, grey-haired woman in her sixties. Perhaps thousands of girls have been helped over Wimbledon's emotional hurdles by this kind woman, who, in the first moment of our meeting, sensed my fright and did her best to put me at ease. Once again, I was tremendously impressed by the facilities and the perfect organization. The dressing-room contained everything a girl might need—even to hairpins, make-up and Cologne. A masseuse stood ready to take the kinks out of aching muscles, while Mrs. Ward told me she would wash and iron my dresses and take care of my shoes. Nothing in the United States approaches this impeccable service.

My reverie in this dreamland was broken by the ringing of the phone. The Press wanted to know when I was coming on the courts for practice, but before I reached the courts there was a new and strange formality. I met Colonel W. J. Legge, the tournament referee, who informed me players were assigned to specific courts for practice on a rigid time schedule. Now I had slips for a court, six brand-new balls, and even ball boys to

'Little Mo' in action on the Centre Court, Wimbledon, while defending her All England Championship title against her compatriot, Doris Hart, in July 1953

*After the presentation by H.R.H. The Duchess of Kent,
Maureen Connolly with the Wimbledon Plate, emble-
matic of world supremacy in women's tennis*

attend me. This, I thought, was a far cry from the days when I was a tiny girl in pigtails, clutching a borrowed racket, fighting tooth and nail to get on a public court in San Diego.

I posed for pictures, frightened still, certain I would be late for practice and somehow throw the court time-table out of gear. Then I rallied with Louise Brough, making a truly spectacular start. I missed the first fast ball she sent, and I missed it completely! (As an aside, may I say I do not like to practise with a formidable opponent. It is my conviction such a session gives her a familiarity with one's game, a chance to probe for chinks in the tennis armour.) We rallied for half an hour. Louise was calm, cool and deadly, knowing every blade of grass as an old friend. For me it was a baffling experience. The grass at Wimbledon gives the ball amazing pace—an effect of hitting the turf, then shooting. I think it takes a minimum of at least a week to become accustomed to it. Then, too, the Slazenger balls are faster and lighter than their American counterpart. I am certain the Press viewed my first efforts with gentlemanly alarm, and later, when Louise and I attempted a set, my play did nothing to enhance my tennis stature. Needless to add, I lost.

The first time I took the centre court was against Angela Mortimer, a fine English player, who, luckily enough for me, was also making her first appearance on this 'outdoor chamber of horrors.' The backdrops seemed miles away, the space on either side of the court appeared acre-like. In our rally, I didn't get in a single ball, or so it seemed. As I took a practice serve, I thought a million eyes were peering at me. (No one in history, as far as I know, has taken the centre court in their stride the first time.) I lost the four games with amazing ease before I finally warmed up and took the match.

After that harrowing match against Susan Partridge, where the voice of the stranger—a stroke of fate—saved me from certain defeat, I faced Mrs. Thelma Long, the Australian champion, with more confidence in the quarter-finals. This confidence was shored up by the arrival of Nelson Fisher just before the match. He bubbled with enthusiasm and friendliness. 'I've

3—FD

read about your shoulder and the bad breaks in the papers,' he told me, then he smiled and added: 'But, Maureen, I want you to go out on that court now . . . and win! I didn't fly all the way over here to see you lose . . . and I *know* you can win!'

That was a lift. From San Diego to London is a long way to travel, and I wasn't going to let Nelson down if I could help it. However, I did manage to lose the first set 7-5. I kept talking to myself (silently, of course) and my tennis improved. Perhaps I am better when I'm behind, as so many have contended. At any rate, I took the second set 6-2, then ran out the third set 6-0.

I raced off the court and the first thing I saw was Nelson's big smile. 'I've really hit my game,' I bubbled. 'Now, I think I have a chance to win the tournament.'

'Of course you have,' he returned. 'You'll win it.' (For Nelson, the possibility of my defeat simply did not exist.)

Memory of a turbulent afternoon at Forest Hills came back when I faced Shirley Fry in the semi-finals. This time there would be no Teach to rescue me between sets. I was on my own, but, at least, I had one conquest over Shirley to bolster my spirits. The first set went badly for me when Shirley ran up a 4-1 lead. I over-hit, made numerous errors, while Shirley played some really fine tennis. I knew many people thought I had been 'lucky' against Shirley at Forest Hills. Now I resolved I'd show them. My hate mounted, my game soared, and I ran off five straight games to take the set, 6-4, in twenty-one minutes.

I fought savagely in the second set, took a 3-1 lead, then I let up momentarily and Shirley pulled up even. I turned on more steam, stamped out her rally and ran her ragged just as she had run me ragged in the second set at Forest Hills. My last shot was a hard-hit backhand, which Shirley missed. I won the set 6-3.

Now I was in the finals. Louise Brough, three times Wimbledon winner, was making a come-back. She had reached the finals by beating Pat Todd, who had played magnificent tennis to eliminate Doris Hart, holder of the title. I was nervous and tense against Louise. I had beaten her at La Jolla, but before coming to Wimbledon she had trimmed me 5-8, 6-2, 6-3, at the Southern California Tennis Championships in Los Angeles.

Louise was making her fifth appearance in the centre court in a finals match, while this was my first. Louise is mistress of every shot in tennis, masterful with the drop, baffling with a cut drive and chop, deadly at the net, and her service is usually powerful. The climax of our match came in the tenth game. Louise led 5-4, and it was then she became nervous. She'd throw up a ball to serve; it wouldn't be tossed right and she'd throw up another. I knew she was becoming weary. It was her service and I wanted to break through, but she fought back bitterly. I had game point three times, before I finally won it, bringing the score to 5 all. The strain was beginning to tell and I took the next two games, winning on my first set point.

Louise called on every ounce of her championship form as we started the next set and she ran up a 2-0 lead. Then my game caught fire, I gambled, shot for the lines and 'went for broke.' I made it 5-2 and 40-0 on my service when Louise made her last gallant stand. She was dead tired, had been bothered by a series of foot faults which had been called against her, but she rose up like a champion in this game. I had three match points, but nothing in my arsenal, neither my hate nor fear, could stem her as she took the game in a truly courageous effort.

I was set to conquer her the next game, and, ironically enough, I made it match point on a tricky drop shot. Then I took the match with a hard drive to her backhand, which she netted.

I was the world's champion—the youngest Wimbledon winner since the fabled English girl, Lottie Dod, captured the classic in 1887 when she was fifteen years old.

Only a few minutes later in my dressing-room I met Nell Hopman, who was to change the course of my life.

CHAPTER NINE

LIFE PACKED A LOT OF THRILLS into 1952 and so much happened I don't know where to begin. After winning Wimbledon, I successfully defended my American title at Forest Hills; I won the Pacific Southwest, scoring a triumph over Shirley Fry; I met Harry Hopman, who became so important to my tennis career; I was given a homecoming parade in San Diego and presented with a horse, but more than anything else, there was romance. I fell in love with Norman Brinker, who was to become my husband.

Strangely enough, neither of my finals victories, either at Forest Hills or Los Angeles, saw my best tennis. In each tournament the semi-finals stood out, a fact commented upon by both the New York and Los Angeles journalists. Although I beat Doris Hart in the finals each time, it was Shirley Fry who ignited the real fireworks.

Forest Hills started off easily in the early rounds. I didn't have a really hard match until the quarter-finals, when I ran into Nancy Chaffee Kiner; she opened up strongly, but didn't sustain her pace. I beat her 6-3, 6-0. Never at a loss for words, Nancy analysed her own game with a devastating remark: 'I played like a plumber.'

In the semi-finals, I faced Shirley Fry. I had beaten her at Wimbledon, and I likewise had taken that harrowing match against her the year before at Forest Hills. Now, I was the champion, and the pressure would be on me. Shirley came on the court with a preconceived battle plan, and in the opinion of many tennis writers had she stuck to her original attack she would have dethroned me. She softballed me, just as Susan Partridge had done at Wimbledon with telling effect. Shirley ran off five straight games to win the first set 6-4.

Highly confident, Shirley opened the second set with a 2-0 lead. Then she began to hit hard, perhaps certain in her mind she could blast me off the court. Now I was getting the kind of balls I liked and in this power duel I knew I could defeat her. I pulled up and made it 2 all. Again, Shirley switched to her soft attack and went ahead 4-2. Then, I managed to bring it to 4-3. At this point, Shirley once more resorted to power. One writer described the rest of the match in a single line : 'Shirley started to drive and she drove herself right out of the match.' I ran off the set 6-4, and in the third set Shirley made numerous errors and I took it 6-1.

'The finals were strictly anti-climactic,' another writer summed it up. I had beaten Doris Hart before and I knew I could do it again. There was no vestige left of my hero-worship. Eleanor Tennant had taken care of that. I was cold, calculating, accurate, powered for the match by my hate and fear. 'Maureen was always master of the situation and the tennis was not particularly thrilling,' was another journalistic comment. I beat Doris 6-3, 7-5.

Almost all tennis champions try for two peaks—Wimbledon and Forest Hills—and the Pacific Southwest Tournament at Los Angeles, which follows Forest Hills, has often seen some surprising let-downs, including the wholesale defeat of the Australian stars, who previously had swept everything before them.

I sometimes failed to play my best in the Pacific Southwest, but this year I think I proved I was a 'clutch player' when the going became the roughest. Shirley Fry was gunning for me and she almost got me. Apparently I had learned nothing at Forest Hills. She took the first set in the semi-finals 6-4.

Now the searing drama of pressure. She led 8-7 in the second set, holding match point at 40-0. Following a good forcing shot, Shirley came to the net to cut off my return and put away the match. I passed her with a cross-court forehand. On the next point, she executed a perfect lob to the baseline. I flew for this one, making a lucky return over my shoulder and Shirley netted a high backhand volley. Once more she had match point, but this was her last one. I hit a cross-court placement and she was running the wrong way!

I knew then that I could pull out the match. Her failure to win four match points was a 'sign.' I turned on heat and power, took three straight games to win 10-8. Shirley let down and tired in the third set, which I took 6-2.

It was after this match an odd thing happened. A man dressed in a neat brown suit came up to me and asked: 'How is Jess?' That's an abbreviation of my mother's first name, which is Jessamine. 'Fine,' I answered absently. 'I'm glad to hear it,' he said, smiled and walked away. He hadn't given me his name; he looked strangely familiar, perhaps I should know who he was, but I didn't. Then I dismissed the incident from my mind.

Again the finals were anti-climactic. I vanquished Doris Hart 6-4, 3-6, 6-1. Here I should add that poor Doris was suffering from a terrible case of blisters and could not cover the court properly.

In America, as everywhere else, a parade is a thing apart, and the old expression 'I'd walk a mile to see a parade' held true for me. Now I was to have a parade in my honour.

The parade began with blaring bands, ticker tape, and all of San Diego, or so it seemed, turned out. It lasted an hour, the sidewalks were lined for a solid mile, every school band in the city participated, every dignitary appeared. Sitting high atop a white convertible, wearing a dress to match the car, and carrying a huge bouquet of roses, I rode up Broadway, the main street of San Diego. Appropriately enough, Nelson Fisher, who had been with me during my big moments of triumph, was sitting with the driver in the front seat. At first I was terribly embarrassed, but this emotion changed to pure joy born of the warmth and magnitude of the tribute. As I looked out over the crowds, I thought to myself: 'No girl in the world has worked harder to become a tennis champion. . . . Perhaps these people know something of the struggle to reach the top.' Had my hate and fear brought me all this? I thought so, then.

The parade ended with a reception in San Diego's beautiful Balboa Park, and it was announced that the San Diego Junior Chamber of Commerce would give me a horse! For as long as I can remember, I had wanted a horse, but never could I afford one, and now, at last, the wish would become a wonderful reality. A 'publicity horse' was given to me then for the sake of the newsreels and photographers. I was to select the one I wanted the next day at the Mission Valley stables. For some reason, this equine 'stand in' shied at my white dress and I had a difficult time even getting close enough to him for the pictures.

I dreamed all night of my new prize and morning was a long time coming, but finally it was time for me to dash down to the stables and pick out my dream charger. Then disappointment took quick hold, as none of the six horses I was shown in any way resembled the steed I had pictured in my mind. I had wanted a golden palomino. Morley Golden, a horseman and construction magnate, stood near by and watched disappointment cross my face.

'Maureen,' he said, taking a photograph out of his wallet, 'here is a horse you might like.'

I looked at the picture and fell in love with a beautiful light sorrel gelding with a white blaze, four white stockings and a flaxen mane and tail. He was the closest thing to my dream palomino.

'I'll take him,' I announced hopefully.

So Golden cancelled his appointments for the day, drove me to his ranch and I met Colonel Merryboy, a Tennessee walking horse. The gait of this breed is like no other—so smooth, so steady you might be riding on a cloud.

I wrote about him in the newspaper column I was doing for the *San Diego Union*, but as the glowing adjectives rolled out of my typewriter I was unaware that Colonel Merryboy, such a gentle and sweet animal, would play such a tragic role in my life.

These were golden autumn days and I rode in the mornings at Mission Valley just as I had done before when I had the chance, but now I was astride my very own horse. Oddly enough, Norman Brinker had been riding there for a year, but he rode in the afternoon so our bridle trails had never crossed. My aunt and uncle, Mr. and Mrs. Clarence Schwab, knew Norman, liked him, and suggested I meet him. They were both interested in riding and had admired Norman's horsemanship. He was one of the youngest members of the United States equestrian team, although at the time he was an enlisted man in the Navy.

And so I met Norman. He was tall, dark and handsome, to use the triple cliché, and he had green eyes, a warm and friendly manner; he's an individualist, one of the world's finest horsemen, and his ability to tame a wild colt may have given him the proper background to cope with a headstrong tennis star. Every girl dreams of a Prince Charming, but I was a tennis player, not a potential bride; a stranger even to a can-opener, and I'd heard husbands like to eat. I was no candidate for marriage.

There are two versions to our first meeting. I was pleasant, reticent and demure (my version). Norman contends I riddled him with a barrage of questions (material for my newspaper column) and he was unable to get in a word. Then I watched him warm up a jumper. First he did figure eights and then he took the jumper over the hurdles. I was entranced by Norman's skill and effortless grace.

For the next two days I haunted the telephone, but Norman was never on the other end. I greeted numerous salesmen with a telephonic breathlessness, which chilled instantly. Finally I grew weary of the vigil, decided to go to a movie alone, and it was then, of course, Norman phoned and asked for a date. Mom, who knew her daughter, accepted for me.

Our first evening together was interesting but unromantic. Norman showed some slides of U.S. Olympic riding scenes to a group of horse enthusiasts. On the way home, we stopped for a bite to eat and I grilled Norman at length (more column material). I found he had played on the high school tennis team in New Mexico, where he was born, so I promptly made a tennis date. This almost proved my undoing. I had a golden opportunity to make him look good on the court, but a mean streak flared up and I ran him ragged with drop shots and lobs. His embarrassment was heightened by the taunts of a group of small fry, who piped: 'Gee, we feel sorry for you.'

We stopped at my home for tea and I tried my best to salvage the situation by turning on all the personality and charm I possessed. I also made more notes for my column, and eventually I did write an interesting piece on him.

Well, the master strategy was simple. I had my tennis, Norman had his horses, and we would be good pals, nothing more. My heart, however, wasn't tuned in to this platonic wavelength. I grew fonder of Norman all the time; I was falling in love, but I didn't know it.

Meanwhile Perry T. Jones had arranged an Australian tour for me that year and he did it with several shrewd purposes in mind. He thought Harry Hopman, captain of the Australian Davis Cup team, would be a perfect coach for me. Then, too, he believed that Nell, who is Harry's wife, would be an excellent companion and chaperone; she would act as a Press buffer and I would have no more unfortunate experiences with journalists on tour. At first, I was less than enthusiastic. I was tired and stale with playing so much tennis, but I had met Harry Hopman at Forest Hills and liked him at once. 'Maureen,' he had told me, 'if you come over, I may be able to help you with some of your strokes.' Recalling this promise, I decided to go.

Now, a few days before I had to leave, I became sad at the prospect. One evening Norman asked me: 'Maureen, what do you really think of me?' My reply shot back with involuntary suddenness: 'I'm crazy about you, Norm.' This produced a slight case of masculine shock. Then, on the eve of my departure, when Norman said good night, he put his arms around me. I kissed him—our first kiss after so many weeks. Again he was taken by surprise. At least, tennis had taught me the art of attack.

This was our first parting, the first of many, and it may be that absence makes the heart grow fonder, but I don't recommend it. Love by letters can be a two-way trial, but this separation didn't bring the grief that was to come later.

No, this was a time of roses . . . of adventure . . . and of a wonderful friendship with Nell and Harry Hopman.

CHAPTER TEN

NELL AND HARRY HOPMAN are my two knights in shining
and untarnished tennis armour. I should like you to meet them
both, because it was Nell who brought me a great happiness,
while Harry lifted my game to its highest peak. There will be a
spot of travel here as I was making my first Australian tour and
the sights at times were more thrilling than the tennis.

Now I should like to introduce Nell, whom I met first at
Wimbledon just after I had won the finals. I was alone in the
dressing-room and Nell saw an emotionally exhausted little girl,
almost in tears. Instinctively she knew how I felt, understood the
turmoil I had gone through, and her congratulations were sincere
and from the heart. Nell had been an international tennis star,
won a large share of the Australian titles, and knew the stress
and strain that is so much a part of championship tennis. In
addition, Nell is highly intelligent, with a quick, keen mind;
she is cultured, a woman at ease in the world, but more than
anything else she has deep sympathy and understanding. Our
relationship was to become as close as mother and daughter.
Nell had no children of her own, and as she helped me 'grow up'
I became almost her own daughter. We toured the world together, seeing the special wonders of many countries.

I was 'raw material' for Nell; I lacked social finesse, and my
temper, which I kept throttled on the courts, was apt to flare
up off them. I was not fully aware of the fact that a champion
is expected to go to various official functions, that acceptance is
mandatory, and I, to a degree, was an 'ambassador' for my
country. Nell, however, knew the social rules, and further she
decided my temper was so much excess baggage. Perry Jones
had stipulated Nell, one of his best friends, was to be in complete command. Julie Sampson, a fellow Californian from San

Marino, the United States Junior champion and a truly lovely girl, was making the tour with me and would play in all the tournaments.

En route to Australia, we stayed four days in Honolulu. We were given a huge and magnificent suite at the Royal Hawaiian Hotel, where we were scheduled to play several exhibition matches. The custom of presenting a pineapple to each guest proved the gastronomic undoing of Julie. Nell wasn't hungry, I dislike pineapple, but Julie tackled all three, promptly becoming *hors de combat*.

I was poised and ready for the lovely beach in front of the hotel, but Nell insisted we first call on George and Vi Pebbles, the tennis pros at the Royal Hawaiian. Here was our first clash. Nell proved a firm and formidable foe, winning the argument in fifteen hectic minutes. George and Vi were charming, I liked them at once, and subsequently our friendship deepened. A crowd had gathered on the courts, but Julie was in no shape for tennis and I wanted to relax. Vi suggested shopping, and the allure of the beach faded. We toured Honolulu on a shopping spree; I bought two dresses, while Nell, who can't resist a new handbag, stocked up.

Honolulu is one of the most beautiful places in the world with an atmosphere that's languid and lazy—the sort of life I had never lived—and I enjoyed every second of it. Suitably enough, a man named Mo was chosen for me as a surfboard instructor and I finally learned to ride one standing up, although my lack of control made me a marine menace. Julie, an accomplished water-skier, became an expert at once.

Four days passed in a happy haze before it was time to leave. It was then I discovered I had lost the return portion of my plane ticket! This created a furore, first class. Nell pulled all strings, finally fixed it so another ticket would be issued in Australia. We were winging our way in the airliner shortly afterwards when I rummaged through my bag looking for lipstick. You guessed it. I pulled out the ticket, let it flutter and cried: 'Here it is, Nell!' Innate gentility prevented her bopping me over the head with a racket, but, come to think of it, she didn't have one handy.

As in England, tennis enjoys immense popularity in Australia —much more so than in the United States—and we were met by a large crowd at the Sydney airport. Here I received my first introduction to Australian flies. There must be billions of them —all possessing tremendous sticking power. In time one develops an automatic brushing action, a built-in involuntary reflex, but the flies were annoying at first and a nuisance during matches. I sprayed on a repellent, but it wore off, and it would have been a bit awkward to have held a racket in one hand and a spray-gun in the other.

Although at first the Australian tour had not been an appealing prospect—I had been tired and over-tennised when it was first suggested—the clincher had come for me at Forest Hills when I first met Harry Hopman and he had offered to help me. I knew what a great coach he was and I thought this might be an excellent chance to improve my game.

Hopman is, as you know, the non-playing captain of the Australian Davis Cup team, an internationally controversial figure, often a storm centre, but if 'Hop' ever needs a witness I should like to take the stand on his behalf. He is, in my opinion, one of the all-time great coaches. I speak from experience, not hearsay.

Hop wants to win. At the moment of writing he has coached the Australian team to four Davis Cup triumphs in five years! Today, the Aussies look invincible and nowhere on the tennis horizon are their conquerors in sight. Hop is interested in results and he gets them. He believes perfect physical condition is essential for championship tennis. He demands it. He has been criticized for imposing a tyrannically Spartan training routine, yet I have been under this rigorous regimen, and because of it I reached the pinnacle of my game. To me he was a source of great inspiration.

As you may have read, Russia is furiously building courts and planning a world-wide tennis assault. I do not know if

Soviet master spys were given a global assignment to ferret out 'tennis secrets,' but I do know the Kremlin wrote to Hop asking for a detailed, hour-by-hour breakdown of his teaching and training methods. It may be presumed the Soviets want to win, and it likewise can be assumed they sought what they considered the best advice in the world.

The day he steps down will be bleak and sad for Australian tennis. Yet he is often under a drum-fire of criticism, and while he shrugs it off with 'I see I made the papers again,' these attacks make me boil.

Hop, a journalist with the *Melbourne Herald*, has been accused of 'holding out' stories for his own paper; not permitting tennis writers into the dressing-rooms before important matches. From experience, I know he leaned backwards to be fair about news. As for the other accusation, his first consideration has been for his team. No player likes to be distracted before an important match.

He has been blamed because the Australian team is over-tennised. The fault here, I think, lies with the Australian Lawn Tennis Association, which receives a cut of foreign gates, thus benefiting financially from long schedules. I agree that fewer tournaments and better spacing would be preferable.

My introduction to Hop's training routine came with shocking impact shortly after we arrived in Sydney. He asked if I would like to train with the boys, and naturally I was thrilled with the prospect, certain even a brief exposure would put me on edge for the next day's matches. Road work came first. Julie, who has long legs and is an easy and graceful runner, had no difficulty. I had to sprint occasionally to keep up; exhaustion was setting in, and only fond thoughts of a long hot tub and an equally long rest kept me going. When we finished our run, I was poised for retreat, but Ken MacGregor noticed me and asked: 'Just where are you going?' I explained, and he treated me to a superior smile and announced: "Callisthenics come next, you know.'

And they did, but that was not all. Hop wanted me to

master rope-skipping with all the skill of a boxer. I believe I finally got my hot tub, but I know I do not remember my head touching the pillow. The morning aftermath was awful. I had difficulty getting out of bed—my legs were tied in knots, my muscles drum-tight. Nell took one horrified look, summoned a doctor, who arrived with the foulest-smelling ointment I'd ever seen, but at least it kept me off crutches.

If the gallery that afternoon came to see a champion, I surely didn't resemble one, and, although I managed to win, my tennis must have been a sorry spectacle. But gradually, under Hop's training, I became so fit that I could play all day, and I had the certain knowledge that none of my opponents would come on the court in such superb condition as I.

Hop became convinced that if I were on my game and in top physical condition, I would be virtually invincible. He seldom worried about my opponents, but I did not share his supreme confidence. I could endow a first-round foe with all the best shots of Lenglen and Wills, plus a few added ones which my imagination might conjure up.

Hop often said I was a perfectionist. 'I always thought,' he remarked, 'Rosewall was the world's worst perfectionist. But now I know you are!' Although it is true I never became satisfied with my game, I considered myself a warrior more than anything else, but there could have been a shade of truth in Hop's observation.

Hop is one of the nicest, kindest, most considerate men I have ever known. He is in his late fifties, still plays a fine game of tennis and was an Australian Davis Cup star from 1928 till 1938. He and Nell met Fred Perry and Dorothy Round in the 1935 Wimbledon mixed doubles finals, losing after a hard battle. Hop would practise with me if he were exhausted. There have been times when he sharpened my game, although his corns were killing him.

It is my opinion that only when Hop is on court does the Australian Davis Cup team reach its potential. In Davis Cup matches, the two non-playing captains sit on opposite sides of the court. The players, as they change courts, talk to the captains. Hop is a master tactician; he knows exactly what his team should do, and his presence is invaluable.

If the players didn't sometimes resent his rigid supervision, they wouldn't be boys. They know, however, he can bring them to the peak essential for their finest effort. Hop, incidentally, imposes a midnight curfew and a non-swearing rule. Violations bring fines which go into a players' fund for flowers and chocolates for kind hostesses.

Hop's coaching and my sightseeing were high-spots of the Australian tour for me. I won all the Australian singles titles, and in most of the finals I played against Julie. The girls do not compare with the Aussie boys—their tennis is on the social side, with time off for tea. I love both social tennis and tea, but certainly they shouldn't be confused with championship tennis. The Australian courts, by the way, are perfectly maintained, the grass is excellent, but often there is a wind and it becomes necessary to compensate. Because of the extreme heat the matches are often played in the early evening.

Australia truly was wonderful—a land of happy memories—so let's hit a few high-lights. Two baby koala bears had been born in the Lone Pine sanctuary in Brisbane, so it was arranged for Julie and me to christen them, naming them after ourselves. The baby koala clings tightly to its mother's back, so we were given the mother bears and asked to pour a drop or two of ginger beer over the babies. My mother bear took one sniff of the ginger beer, and being a true Australian wanted all of it, and this posed a real handling problem.

After the christening, I wandered over to a cage where some medium-sized tannish-coloured dogs were kept. One of them came up to me, looked friendly enough and I decided to pet him. 'Don't!' came like a shot from the keeper. I jerked my hand back, and this was my rather rude introduction to the wild dingo dog, a savage animal, which will attack even man. These dogs run in packs, kill sheep and are a general nuisance.

It was hot in Australia when we were there, and, of course,

Julie and I looked forward to the beaches and swimming. We had another rude awakening. The boys on the Australian team described the sharks native to the waters and the size of the *Queen Mary* paled by comparison. Australians take sharks as a matter of course, but there have been many tragic accidents. Julie and I didn't venture much beyond ankle-depth. Swimmers are cautioned to stay in compact groups and are supposed to go no deeper than their thighs. Lifeguard towers and even helicopters maintain a sharp patrol, and when a shark is sighted a bell tolls in the tower and everyone scrambles for the beach. Needless to add, Julie and I attempted no surfboard riding. However, it is done and really is a feat because the waves are mountainous, pounding in with sledge-hammer force.

Nell, who knew the director of the famous Sydney Zoo, arranged a plush tour for us. In the aquarium I saw what was believed to have been the largest sting-ray ever caught, and we looked at this monster at point-blank range. No, I didn't try to pet him, or even make friends with a passing giant nurse shark, who paused and eyed us speculatively as a possible between-meals snack.

Later, my back to a cage, I stood and talked to the director, when suddenly a strange face leaned down next to mine. I leaped four feet. The director smiled, then formally presented Henry, a young friend of his, who loved cookies. I held a package of them in my hand, and naturally Henry wanted some. So Henry, a giraffe, became a friend.

One morning in Melbourne, when Nell wasn't with us, Hop arranged for me to meet Jack Purtell, the famous Australian jockey. I, of course, was thrilled. Australia has produced many great racehorses, and in San Diego they still talk of Phar Lap, who in his one start and triumph at Agua Caliente impressed many veteran horsemen as the greatest thoroughbred ever seen on the North American continent—superior even to the legendary American champion Man o' War.

We met Jackie at a training track and he wanted to know if I would like to ride. Naturally I couldn't wait, but there was the slight matter of costume. I was wearing a tight grey skirt, strictly impossible riding attire. I looked at Harry's trousers.

'No you don't,' he said, quickly reading my mind.

'Yes, I do !' I came back.

The upshot was Harry and I retired behind two large trees. I got far the better of the fit, thanks to Hop's belt, but we were a humorous sight, especially Hop, who couldn't get the skirt properly zipped and it hung askew. Although this wasn't planned for publicity, the photographers had a field day, the pictures making all of the Australian newspapers and even *Time* magazine in the United States.

Jackie selected a lead pony who had speed, spirit and a will of his own. He held the halter to see how I would get along, but when he let go my mount was off for the races. We romped through a garden at full gallop and this charger either had a hard mouth or I weak arms, because I couldn't slow him down at bit. To the right, I saw a high wall, much too high for him to leap, so I headed straight for it and as we neared the obstacle he put out his front feet and skidded to a true polo-pony stop.

Now my mount had worked off his excess energy he felt happy and was willing to be a good boy. I was ready for more, but then I saw Jackie sprinting towards me on foot, his face sheet-white.

'If anything had happened to you, Maureen,' he panted, 'I never would forgive myself.'

Hop thought it was all a huge joke and so did I.

'Wait until I tell Nell,' I laughed.

'Don't do that,' Hop implored. 'She'd murder me.'

So we kept this a deep, dark secret from Nell for almost two years. Finally I was laughing to myself about it one evening and broke down and confessed to Nell.

Well, the afternoon of my ride, we went to the Melbourne track and watched Jackie ride. He was truly great, every bit as good as Hop had claimed.

Hop was determined I should not leave Australia without

having met an aborigine, and, naturally Hop, who knew everyone, had a friend who was a member of this vanishing race. Incidentally, they are used largely to track down escaped criminals in the rugged bush country, which they know far better than any Aussie.

Our aborigine spoke English! He was dark, wiry, muscular and a marvellous hunter and tracker. Hop thought Julie and I should at once become adept with boomerang and spear, believing, no doubt, feminine accomplishments should include providing dinner as well as preparing it. Julie quickly became our boomerang champion, but you should have seen Hop's friend! He had the most remarkable sense of timing I have ever seen. He threw the boomerang, and, as it winged its way back, I was ready to run, certain we would be hit. Our aborigine smiled, pointed to a spot about five feet from us and said: 'It will land there.' It did!

To really comprehend the immensity of Australia one should fly over it, and on the trip from Adelaide to Perth we saw huge stretches of barren and arid land, dotted at intervals by stations, or ranches as we say in America.

Nell, Julie and I visited a tremendously large station outside Victoria. It stretched for hundreds of miles and I don't know how many thousands of sheep and cattle grazed there. Naturally I wanted to ride, but Nell, never keen about my riding, personally selected the mount, a docile animal, quite suitable for a baby. The terrain, by the way, was absolutely flat. No mishaps here.

Another time, at a ranch outside Mexico City, I planned a ride, but Nell promptly vetoed the idea.

'If the Mexicans ride the way they drive automobiles,' she told me, 'I don't trust their horses.'

Our Australian tour wouldn't be complete without a description of Christmas. This, in the United States, is traditionally a time for snow and sleighs, and although in San Diego we have no snow, nothing quite compared to Christmas in Melbourne. It was almost one hundred degrees in the shade! We were the guests of Sir Norman Brooks, who had been one of Australia's great tennis players, and was then president of the Australian Lawn Tennis Association. He has a lovely estate, bordered by a secluded inlet.

The turkey was divine, the weather stifling, and neither Julie nor I could whip up much appetite. Swimming was the only thing really appealing, but this was a mistake. We went to the inlet with Ken Rosewall, who detoured on a marine expedition of his own. He caught a baby octopus! But as he approached, Julie and I took one look and fled!

Purposely I have saved the most important event of my Australian tour until now, and it truly marked a turning-point in my life as surely as any signpost. Nell and I were sitting one night in our hotel suite in Sydney, when for the very first time I told the complete truth about myself. I held back nothing. I made no excuses. To be great, I had to hate, to feel fear, and, as I high-lighted some of my triumphs, when these emotions lifted me, Nell listened in horrified silence, stunned and unwilling to believe. Here was a fantastic tale I was making up. This could not be true of the girl she loved as her own child, but as I poured out my story Nell saw the pain and trouble in my face. She knew it was true and her deep compassion came like a flood.

We talked for hours and my burden grew lighter. Nell's shoulders were broad and she shirked nothing. Now it was her problem too; she was no fair-weather friend in this turbulent emotional sea. She decided exactly what to do and there would be no deviation from the course she set. My tennis, she told me, would not suffer, if I cast off hate and fear. I did not agree, for this would be throwing away my two most potent weapons. Nell did not tell me only an emotional crack-up lay ahead of me, but she knew it.

She demanded a fast and irrevocable break. I was to play Julie the next day and I liked Julie—off the court—and although I had never lost to her, I still hated, still felt fear, when I faced her across the net. Tomorrow it would be different. Nell pleaded with me to play my best against Julie, to enjoy the match, to keep the thought uppermost that Julie was a friend, not an enemy, and there could be no hate, no fear.

And so another strange drama unfolded, a play within a play, performed for an audience of two. Nell's instructions were the most difficult I ever had. I called upon every fibre of my will-power and determination to carry them out. Instinctively, I wanted to hate Julie, and I wanted to feel fear much as the masochist might want the lash. I strangled these emotions, looked across at Julie, concentrating on the fact that she was a lovely girl and a friend. My tennis was by instinct, reflexes, not design, but suddenly I knew I was playing wonderful tennis. Miraculously, a swelling exultation rose within me, a new, different and glorious emotion. For the first time in my tournament career I really enjoyed the game, thoroughly, completely and to the very hilt. Julie, concentrating on her hard-hitting game, was unaware then or later that I was winning the hardest emotional struggle of my life.

For this great gift, Nell will never outlive my devotion and gratitude.

CHAPTER ELEVEN

LOVE AND TENNIS were interwoven in 1953. This was the year when I became the world's first woman 'Grand Slam' champion. It was also the year of my greatest Wimbledon, where I approached the mythical 'perfect game,' and it was the year, too, of the Coronation—the most stirring sight of my life. Yes, it was a time of love, fun, travel and conquest—a truly glorious year—and now there was no hate, no fear, and new and wonderful vistas opened for me in tennis.

I returned from Australia to San Diego, and no actress rehearsed an 'entrance' more than I on the last hundred miles of the flight. Wearing mascara for the first time, I would walk down the steps from the air-liner, give the photographers a sophisticated and enigmatic smile, then melt into Norman Brinker's arms. Mata Hari, I am sure, would have been several lengths behind this performance. The air-liner landed. My entrance began beautifully, then suddenly collapsed. Norman wasn't there. He was on duty.

Then, in my pique, I rehearsed a new meeting at home, accentuated by my cool and casual manner. My opening line would be: 'So nice to see you again.' This to be accompanied by a friendly handshake. Nothing more. Norman came. I dived into his arms. My heart couldn't read the stage directions. Time fled happily as our romance deepened.

It seemed I had hardly arrived before I was to leave on a European tour—Italy, France and then Wimbledon. It was on the eve of my departure that Norman proposed, if one could call it that. He gave me a large amethyst ring, then vaguely mentioned something about: 'When we get married.' I shrieked: 'What?' He smiled and asked softly: 'We are going to get married, aren't we?' My 'Of course, darling,' volleyed back. We planned to make a formal announcement when I returned from Wimbledon in July.

My tennis did not soar in Rome. I may have been having too much fun seeing the sights with Nell Hopman and Julie Sampson, who were with me again. I lost to Doris Hart in the finals of the Italian championships. No alibi. She was just playing wonderful tennis.

Then came Paris, and now, if I could win the French championship, I would have the second leg on my 'Grand Slam' try, with the English and American crowns still to be won. Don Budge, by the way, was the only man ever to hold these titles at the same time. Susan Partridge rose up again and almost proved my Nemesis before I reached the finals. She had, by the way, just married Philippe Chatrier, editor and publisher of the French magazine *Tennis de France*. Marriage, if anything, improved Susan's game, and I certainly loomed as no terror on the courts for her. She softballed me down the middle with such effectiveness that she took the first set 6-3, and was leading in the second set 2-0. At this point I turned on every bit of pressure I could muster—I had to win—and slowly I cut down Susan as she started to tire. I won the match 3-6, 6-2, 6-2. Winning the finals against Doris Hart was a little easier, as I managed this in straight sets 6-2, 6-4, to become the French champion.

Now, it was on to London and the big goal was my first defence of my Wimbledon crown. The finals, against Doris Hart, were to mark the zenith of my career. In the early rounds of Wimbledon, I was not playing my best tennis. My ground strokes—the foundation of my game—were not working right. In contrast, Doris floated through her early matches, playing great and flawless tennis, doing absolutely nothing wrong. I had, however, beaten Shirley Fry 6-1, 6-1, in the semi-finals, but Shirley was playing the worst tennis of her career.

Harry Hopman, who was coaching me, wanted my game to sky-rocket for the finals, and there was only one way to achieve that—work. So we were set for a practice session at eleven-forty-five at the Queen's Club. This would be on the boards, which are, of course, faster than grass; the added speed gives an excellent preparation for match play as it sharpens one's reflexes. Hop had arranged for Mervyn Rose, a member of the Australian team, to practise with me. I slugged the first few into the backdrop just as hard as I could. This reflected my earlier coaching under Eleanor Tennant, who thought when I felt nervous and upset this would get it out of my system. It did, although Hop viewed the demonstration in puzzled silence.

Hop's routine for me went like this : he and Rose would be at the net volleying, chasing me from one side of the back court to the other. Then our positions would be reversed, although I didn't chase them anywhere. They would mix hard drives with overhead shots. Next, all three of us would be at the net for a swift volley session. I would finish off by practising my serve. Rose would make the return and I would go for a placement.

Through this, Hop kept yelling, 'Go for your shots,' which is the equivalent of the U.S. Army's 'Go for broke.' Hop believed this the best style of attack for me, the only way I could reach the pinnacle of my game. I think he was absolutely right. Others contend this is too dangerous, too chancy, the risks too great, but my whole game was centred upon a hard, daring offensive, shooting for the lines and corners.

Despite the fact that now my game was not quite clicking, Hop would not advocate my taking it easier, playing it safer, but continued his 'Go for your shots, Maureen.' Incidentally, I consider this routine of Hopman's to be the best in tennis. Well, practice was over at twelve-fifteen; I took a hot tub for about five minutes to relax my muscles and it felt simply wonderful.

Now, the centre court! At one-thirty I went out on the court and had a short knock-up or rally with Ken Rosewall, another member of the Australian team. This was an easy fifteen-minute practice session designed solely to loosen up my arm and limber up my muscles. Just after I finished, Fred Perry, the former world's champion, who also writes about tennis, dropped by and said jokingly : 'I just watched Doris and she's hitting the ball well.' Then he smiled and added : 'You don't seem to be hitting in the centre of your racket, Maureen.' Fred, of course, was absolutely right, although he was merely teasing me. However, I've always had the philosophy of show business : a poor dress rehearsal means a good performance. I kept that in mind then.

Now, so you may better understand the match, I should like to tell you of the dream I have always had of playing a perfect game. Tennis players scoff at such an ambition, contending the very nature of the game prevents its accomplishment. I disagree. There are special 'ground rules,' so to speak, and within this framework such a game is possible. Here I mean a perfect game—the finest one can play—within the limits of one's ability, a game in which no errors are committed, and by errors I mean blunders, not errors which are forced on one by an excellent shot achieved by the opponent. As I always went for the lines, for me the perfect game would be one where I hit each ball within one inch of the line. In this mythical game, each stroke works perfectly, each ball is hit hard and with confidence, placed perfectly. In such a game, the cold digits of the score mean nothing.

Now, we start. Time had run backwards. Across the court was my idol—the nicest and most charming girl in tennis and my dear friend. I felt no hate, no fear, not a vestige of either, but my determination to win was as high as Mount Everest. Although some 40,000 tennis fans had come to Wimbledon that day, and perhaps 17,000 were watching us on the centre court, the match, as far as Doris and I were concerned, might just as well have been played on a desert isle, with only the waving palms as spectators. Our concentration was absolute, neither of us conscious of anything except the match.

Doris played the greatest tennis of her career and so did I. We slugged and 'went for broke' and the difference between us was so marginal as to be non-existent. I won the match 7-5, 8-6, but the points tally tells a far more graphic story. One point separated us in the first set, one in the second set! This was the closest I was ever to come to my 'perfect game.' Although I made a few careless errors, the total of my errors—blunders and forced ones—was less than the placements I earned, which in itself is remarkable.

As we walked off the court together, Doris said: 'Maureen, this is the first time in my life I have lost a match and still felt as though I had won it.' If ever a player deserved a 'dead heat,' if ever there should have been two winning awards for the same match, this was it. For me, it was a tremendous win. I had played the finest tennis of my life, my game soared, and to have won against such a great adversary, at the very height of her game . . . it's a thrill beyond description. And I had won without hate, without fear.

I was not alone in believing this match might take its place in Wimbledon legend. Here are a few quotes:

'It was a privilege to be a spectator . . . it must have been one of the greatest women's matches ever played. . . . And a postscript to a gallant loser. Without the great heart of Doris there would have been no real final this year.' (David Jack in the *Empire News*.)

'They saw not only a match magnificent, but the best tennis of the fortnight.' (Alan Toby in the *Sunday Express*.)

'The all-American final in which Miss Maureen Connolly beat Miss Doris Hart will go down in history as one of the best women's matches ever played anywhere. In an experience which goes back to the 1910 Wimbledon, I do not remember there to have been a better one. It was the perfect pattern of how the game should be played.' (Neville Deed in *The Racquet*.)

Suddenly I was paged for an overseas phone call, and I took it in Duncan MacAulay's office. Nelson Fisher was calling from San Diego to congratulate me and I was thrilled to hear his voice. Just as we were finishing, Nelson remarked casually that Norman was being shipped out. I was stunned and had difficulty finishing our conversation coherently. Now I wouldn't see Norman when I returned home. My tears came in a flood when

I put down the receiver. There was a coat hanging up, fashionable and expensive I'm sure, but I buried my head in it and wept inconsolably. Marie Bumpus, secretary to Duncan MacAulay, viewed my behaviour with alarm, heightened by the fact I was crying into the Duchess of Kent's coat and might ruin it. But I was oblivious, and I would have cried into the Queen's coat had it been hanging there.

Now I was scheduled to play doubles, but all I wanted to do really was cry and feel sorry for myself. Julie Sampson and I took the court against Doris Hart and Shirley Fry. It was a slaughter. We were cut to ribbons, losing 6-0, 6-0. I'm far from the world's best doubles player, but really I'm not that bad, and I was no help to Julie at all. This, of course, is not offered as an alibi. Doris and Shirley could have beaten us easily on the best day we ever had, but this wasn't it.

'Maureen, I don't know whether we should laugh or cry,' Julie said to me. 'This must have been the shortest match in Wimbledon history.'

I returned to the hotel with Nell and immediately placed phone calls to Norman and Mom. When I finally got through to Norman, he told me he'd received his orders two weeks previously and he would be at sea for five months. I was desolate, but even so it gave me a tremendous lift to talk to him. His letters had been so light and gay; he knew, of course, how upset I would have been had I known he was to be shipped out.

Now, let's take our magic carpet to the Coronation! Not in my wildest dreams did I come close to picturing what a magnificent event it would be. Nell was determined we should see it, but we had no tickets—a fact which didn't slow her in the least. She went to work in a hurry, and, after much effort, managed to get a pair. These, I later discovered, cost $500. There simply isn't any American price comparison I can make, but neither, of course, is there a comparable event in my country. The tickets, by the way, were the gift of a rich tennis enthusiast, who learned from one of Nell's friends of our plight.

Nell routed me out of bed at 5.30 a.m. We had to hurry!

I kicked like a yearling steer, but once we were outside I understood the reason for speed. The crush was like nothing I had ever seen—far worse than New York at the rush hour. Walking was much faster than taking a taxi, but even so our progress was painfully slow.

Our seats were wonderful! We had a perfect view from the ledge of a department store, which overlooked the Queen's return route from Westminster Abbey to Buckingham Palace. Our tickets entitled us to breakfast, luncheon and tea, plus the privilege of a ringside TV seat inside. Thus we would have a video view of the actual Coronation.

Enthusiasm was electric and infectious. One could feel the mounting fervour among the happy throngs. It was something I have experienced nowhere else in the world. I am certain any American in my place would understand what the Royal Family means to the British Empire. It is something that cannot be explained in words, at least, not mine.

The first part of the procession began passing our vantage-point at two-thirty and the Queen would pass by at four o'clock. Naturally I had my camera, an extra supply of film, but the temptation to shoot everything was great. I have never seen such pomp and pageantry, with every nation in the world represented in what I imagine was the most lavish spectacle in modern history.

Suddenly, in the distance, there came a deafening roar, a sound so unique, so special, I cannot describe it. The Queen! Excitement sky-rocketed. Nell was screaming and delirious with joy. I found myself yelling, cheering, and I'm sure quite as thrilled as any British subject.

I looked skyward and I was crushed. It started raining. I would get no pictures of the Queen. The weather, by the way, had been foul for several days, but this was the really stunning meteorological blow. My camera was loaded and I was ready. Then, as the Queen's coach drew near, a minor miracle occurred. The rain thinned, then stopped altogether! I clicked a frantic shutter and got some truly wonderful snaps.

The greys drawing the Queen's coach were the most beautiful I had ever seen—each truly a 'picture horse.' The golden coach far surpassed even the one I had fashioned in my dreams for Cinderella. I caught a fleeting glimpse of the beautiful Queen as she looked out and smiled at the throng.

As the Queen passed by, the roar of her subjects must have reached the stars! No one made more noise or was more enthusiastic than Nell or I. That evening, my emotions still in the clouds, I had a sudden sickening thought. The first time I had come to London, I might have had an audience with the then Princess Elizabeth. A leading journalist suggested it could be arranged, but the time would have been 11 a.m. That would have meant no practice. I was, as I have told you, going through a tremendously turbulent emotional period, my shoulder was giving me constant trouble, and I wanted to win Wimbledon more than anything else in the world. So I had declined the possible audience. That night of the Coronation I never regretted a childish decision more.

I had a wonderful surprise when I returned to San Diego. Norman was waiting for me! He had wangled a delay in his orders and now we would be together briefly before he shipped out. The night before he left, he drove me to Balboa Park, a large moon broke through the tall trees in fractured facets of light, there was romance in the air. This would be the moment he would slip a diamond ring on my finger, and for this occasion I had a flowery speech ready. Norman put the twinkling ring on my finger, and I was so ecstatically happy I forgot my speech. Only a devoted kiss served as my acceptance, and the ring was especially wonderful because I knew Norman had worked nights to earn the money for it.

He sailed and my heart sailed with him. I left for Chicago and New York, not particularly keen about either prospect. At River Forest, a suburb of Chicago, I was to play in the National Clay Court championships. I met Althea Gibson, a splendid Negro player, in the finals, defeating her 6-4, 6-4.

After my exciting Wimbledon win, everything else was something of a let-down—even to winning my third consecutive national title at Forest Hills. In that tournament I lost only twenty games in twelve consecutive winning sets. However, I had one unfortunate experience, and that came in the quarter-finals against Althea Gibson. She was, as you may know, the first Negro ever to play at Forest Hills, and some people took a dim view of this. Not I. It is my conviction that any championship tournament would become a travesty if a great player were barred for reasons of colour or race. I liked Althea and our relationship had been friendly. I told her before the tournament began how happy I was she was playing in it and I wished her luck.

Our match was a nightmare. She foot-faulted repeatedly. I won one game at love without returning a single ball. This wasn't tennis, and no one wants to win or even play in a match like this. Although there were two foot-fault judges—a man and a woman—only the woman called the infractions. Why the other judge didn't call them I shall never know. Perhaps he wanted to get on with the match and quiet the boos and catcalls which were beginning to rise from the crowd.

Althea asked the woman judge what she was doing wrong. This, by the way, is perfectly proper. 'You are stepping on the line,' the judge replied. Althea continued this infraction and the foot-faults were promptly called. She was hurting no one but herself. In all modesty, I was a dangerous opponent for her even under the most favourable circumstances, but with this repeated loss of points she held absolutely no winning chance.

I won the first set 6-2. Althea's foot-faulting continued into the second set. As we changed courts I boiled over. 'Althea, either play or default,' I told her. 'I have never seen worse sportsmanship.' Hardly had I said this before I realized that Althea was under tremendous strain, and I was sorry I said it.

I won the match quite easily, taking the second set 6-3. I was never more happy to have one end. I have no explanation of Althea's conduct nor do I know what stress she may have been under. It is quite possible she felt she had been singled out and may have thought she had been a victim of over-officiating.

In the semi-finals I encountered little difficulty, breezing through 6-1, 6-1, against Shirley Fry, who was still far below her best, while my attack clicked perfectly.

Once more it was Doris Hart in the finals, but it was not the same Doris who had opposed me at Wimbledon. Now she definitely was over-tennised. I broke her service in the very first game and now she was no longer quite the formidable foe she had been. I took the first set 6-2.

In the second set I had Doris 5-2. Then she made a bold and glorious stand, and a crowd of 12,000 roared encouragement to her as she came up and I led by a scant game, 5-4. The crowd was tense now; the pressure was on as I served. I made it 15-0 when Doris netted a shot. I reached 30-0 on a service ace. Then, on a placement, I made it 40-0. In our next rally I smashed a forehand cross-court for an outright placement, taking the game, set and match, 6-2, 6-4. That slashing drive was to be my Forest Hills swan song.

Back home in San Diego stretched the rose-petal road to romance. Norman returned from his cruise and in November 1953 we announced our engagement. Ahead, we thought, lay the happiest time in our lives, but it wasn't to be.

CHAPTER TWELVE

THIS IS A FAREWELL to championship tennis—a glorious good-bye—and so that you may savour the exultation and torment I want you to become the 'Grand Slam' champion. You are nineteen years old. Your title will be at stake in the greatest of all tournaments—Wimbledon. If I can tell this as it happened, then for a brief span of dramatic hours you will be the girl with the Golden Racket. Truly, I hope this vicarious experience will give you a better insight into championship tennis.

Before we take the centre court, where the world's sporting spotlight focuses its hot, searching stare, let us lay the groundwork for 1954, a turbulent year for me, paved with heartbreak.

It began badly. My engagement to Norman Brinker was marked by arguments and reconciliations. I was a Catholic; he a Methodist, and there was a religious conflict. We were going through a trying time, two youngsters growing up, both wanting their own way; each stubborn, both spoiled. Our relationship became strained when we parted in the spring. Norman sailed for Hawaii. I left on tour. Our letters were to become indifferent; we read things between the lines which were not really there at all. Then we were to stop writing.

My tennis began badly, too. Beverly Baker Fleitz beat me at La Jolla Beach and Tennis Club's Invitation 6-0, 6-4. Beverly always seems hot at the beginning of a season and on this day she was a fire-cracker on the court.

Italy did not provide much in the way of competition that year and the top American girls were not playing. I went through five rounds, losing only sixteen games, taking the finals from the English girl, Pat Ward, 6-3, 6-0.

On to Paris, and here I was joined by Harry Hopman, who took one look at my tennis and threw up his hands in horror.

He asked Nell, who had been travelling with me, what had happened to my game. The answer, I imagine, was too much sightseeing and too little competition. Hop fixed that at once, or, at least, he put me under his stern training regimen. I successfully defended my title, defeating the French star, Ginette Bucaille, 6-4, 6-4.

Now, let's go on to Wimbledon. I've always had the ability to endow my opponents, at odd moments, with tremendous prowess. To give you an example of this, I was to meet Angela Buxton, an English girl, whom I had beaten rather easily in a previous match in Paris. Now I was thoroughly convinced the situation would be entirely different. Angela had given out an interview saying she did not fear my game, she expected to win. No newspaper reader gave this prediction more weight than I. Furthermore, her father, a wealthy motion picture producer, had promised her a pier—of all things—if she won, plus $100 for each game she took from me. How could she lose!

Hop simply could not understand or share my alarm, but no foe loomed larger or more formidable than Angela. I went into action with a vengeance, cut loose everything I had, determined at all costs to get the jump. As it turned out, Angela was fighting for points, not games. I beat her 6-0, 6-0, in eighteen minutes, and I can assure you I was the most surprised player at Wimbledon.

Another Wimbledon match I should like to mention was against Betty Rosenquest Pratt, who, remembering our Philadelphia match at Merion when I was sixteen, thought she held an excellent chance against me. She didn't know, because of that match, I had worked hundreds of hours on my short game and now I was primed and really ready for her particular attack. I won, 6-1, 6-1.

'I thought I had a good chance against you, Maureen,' she told me after the match, 'but I hadn't realized how much you had improved.' (Betty, of course, had been the original architect of my improvement against her type of game.)

4—FD

Tension does not set in an hour or two before a Wimbledon final; it takes hold almost twenty-four hours before, and it usually builds steadily towards a centre-court climax, which over the years has taken a full toll of nervous heartbreak. The long London summer twilight faded into night as I returned to Grosvenor House, where I was staying with Nell Hopman. My nerves twanged, I felt edgy, irritable, not a fit companion for man, beast or Nell. However, Nell knew my dark Irish moods and she could always shore up my spirits.

We had dinner at nine-thirty and the *maître d'hôtel*, an ardent tennis fan and a supporter of mine, made the meal a huge success. The American-style salad, which I love, is not always a British speciality, but this night it was a masterpiece, thanks to my friend. It was his contribution towards a victory tomorrow. I had a large steak, too, and, because I was nervous, I drank a tall glass of beer, which has the effect of calming me down.

Nell and I went back to our suite and played gin rummy until midnight. Then I wrote letters. Ordinarily, one might think an earlier bedtime was indicated, but for me it would have been just a sleepless toss. I went to bed about twelve-thirty.

Shortly afterwards I had the nightmare, vivid and real as only an often-repeated bad dream can be. It played like this : I was alone in the waiting-room under the Royal Box at Wimbledon. I knew the Royal Family had arrived, and the entourage included the Duke of Edinburgh, Princess Margaret, the Queen Mother and the Duchess of Kent. (Queen Elizabeth, who does not attend the tennis matches, was never in my dream.)

Next I would hear the Duke and the Queen Mother talking, and I could hear the Duke say clearly : 'Louise Brough is on the court, but where is Maureen?' In my dream, he always delivers this line, changing the name of my opponent to fit the occasion.

This was my cue to scream, beat against the waiting-room door in a futile effort to reach the centre court. Gradually I would realize it was hopeless, I was trapped, no one could hear me. Then there would be a few beats of silence, followed by the far away sound of faint clapping, a signal of the crowd's impatience for the match to start.

As the sound of clapping faded, the next two players in this strange drama of the night would take over. I could hear Colonel John Legge, the tournament chairman, say: 'Well, I presume Maureen isn't here.' This was the cue for Duncan MacAulay, secretary of the All England Lawn Tennis Club, to reply: 'We shall have to default her and give the title to Louise.'

It was then I would awaken, trembling, bathed in a cold sweat, certain I had lost by default. This, by the way, was a two-continent nightmare with American variations at Forest Hills. When my tennis career ended, the nightmare left me, and I have never had it since.

Now, at two o'clock in the morning, I tried again for peaceful sleep, knowing the dream would not recur the same night. I thought of the boy I loved, counted sheep and finally fell into a sound slumber. I was awakened at nine-thirty by the waiter's knock, bringing a large breakfast I had ordered the night before. I promptly devoured two eggs, a bowl of fruit, a large glass of orange juice, toast, coffee cake and coffee. I never eat lunch before an afternoon match, so my breakfast is always hearty.

Then I went to Nell's room and we talked a few minutes before I was to leave for the Queen's Club and a practice session with Harry Hopman and Ken Rosewall.

This was a strange day; somehow I could not get keyed up, although the match had double significance as I had made up my mind to turn professional. However, there had been a stipulation. I must win both Wimbledon and Forest Hills. Although the finals were minutes away, I somehow felt it was just another match, nothing too important. This was in sharp contrast to my other finals matches at Wimbledon. And this was the one time since I had known him when Hop became alarmed and felt keenly I might lose. He did not show his concern; I learned about it later from Nell, but he decided to take the court himself for the final knock-up and kept urging me to 'go for my shots' in a desperate last-minute attempt to get me on a fine edge.

There was a blustery wind sweeping across the centre court, which precluded really fine tennis, blowing with it a series of errors into the match. Louise Brough, I thought, was nervous in the first set; her service lacked its usual power, but she was always dangerous. I won the set 6-2.

In the second set, Louise, a crafty field-marshal on the court, used every shot in her wide assortment, mixed them up, and ran up a 5-2 lead as the crowd began to roar, sensing an upset in the making. I became furious at myself—not Louise—and I knew it was time to unleash everything I had. I blasted every ball as hard as I could and, somehow, took five straight games to win the set, 7-5, and the match.

The last point, sharp and clear in memory, now appears ironic. Hop told me repeatedly to dive for hard balls at the net, but never could I pull it off quite right. On this match point, I dived for one—it looked impossible—but to my amazement I made it! And that was my Wimbledon farewell.

Thus I had performed the 'hat trick'—three Wimbledons in a row—and I had done it without the loss of a single set in the finals. Only four other women, including Louise, a gallant loser, had been able to take the 'big one' three times running, but luck and fate had played their part in my victories.

Now for the third time H.R.H. the Duchess of Kent made the presentation in the centre court, and she gave me a charming smile as I accepted the treasured platter and the cameras clicked. (She didn't know my tears had almost ruined her coat the year before.)

This was the night of the great Wimbledon ball, an evening of infectious gaiety that sweeps one along with it, and for me the night suddenly became alive and glowing when I took down my ball gown. The following is for the girls, definitely not required masculine reading.

Teddy Tinling, who I think is one of the world's greatest designers (and a dear friend), made my clothes. 'I want you in the world's most beautiful ball gown,' he had told me. 'My queen has to look superb.' He scoured England for material; he sent away to Paris for samples before he awakened me one morning with : 'I have found it! I must see you at once!'

He bubbled with enthusiasm, unrolled a sketch to which was pinned tiny swatches of a dark pink nylon net shot with silver thread. I couldn't quite visualize it; anyway, it was too early in the morning for me to generate enthusiasm. Teddy looked at me, momentarily crushed, then, like some sort of master of ceremonies describing the creation of the year, he projected the gown (me into it) with a barrage of adjectives which overwhelmed me. I was sure then it would be breath-taking.

It was. The nylon net was scalloped, falling in rose-shaped tiers, and underneath was the widest hooped taffeta skirt I had ever seen. The gown was strapless and Teddy designed a stole of the same material to go over my shoulders. The final fitting was a nightmare. He demanded I stand motionless for half an hour, while he 'created' in the true Continental manner. I moved once and he jabbed me with a pin. Then I was motionless.

Almost 1,500 people had assembled for the dinner, which precedes the dancing, in the huge and beautifully decorated ballroom of Grosvenor House. It is customary for the Wimbledon winners to make an 'entrance' and I had a slight case of the centre-court jitters as I walked slowly down the spiral staircase while the crowd applauded.

The ordeal, however, was not over. There were congratulatory speeches at dinner, and by tradition each winner makes a five-minute response. Normally I speak rapidly even in casual conversation, but now, gripped by stage fright, my delivery must have sounded like the chatter of a machine gun. I am sure no one understood what I said, nor was I too certain, other than saying what a great player Louise was and what a wonderful coach Harry Hopman was.

The year before, Vic Seixas, the American star who won the men's singles, had spoken after I had made my sixty-second oration. He arose calm and cool, looked at me and smiled, then remarked: 'I have a nine-minute speech—four for Maureen, five for myself.'

Jaroslav Drobny, the men's winner this year in a great triumph, did not know it was customary to 'fill in' for me, but he was a wonderful dancing partner. By custom, the first dance is reserved for the winners of the men's and women's singles, and by tradition this is a waltz. Now, I could waltz. The year before when Vic and I had danced it had been a fox-trot. He told me then: 'If we win next year, Maureen, we had better learn to waltz.' (I took his advice.)

For Drobny, victory had been sweet because he had been seeded eleventh, and his triumph had been tremendously popular. The big throng at the ball burst into spontaneous song: 'For He's a Jolly Good Fellow.' I was told this was the first time such a thing had happened at the ball, and surely Drob deserved it.

Nearly a hundred dances and five glasses of champagne later, I went to bed on a bubbling cloud of happiness and slept an even twelve hours.

'Little girl, you had a busy day.'

CHAPTER THIRTEEN

TRIUMPH AND TRAGEDY came swiftly in 1954 and it came
for both Norman and me. It was a mixture of magic and heartbreak in stories that ran curiously parallel. If I was a champion,
so was Norman, and his athletic feats stand almost without
equal in sports history, and here I shall try to pull our two
stories together and take you behind the Iron Curtain with
Norman.

While I had been on tour in Europe, Norman had been
shipped to Hawaii, which he liked, but he still yearned to return
to the States. There was one chance, a seemingly futile hope,
but he seized it. The United States was preparing its 1954
Modern Pentathlon team, its members to be chosen from the
armed services, and of the thousands of Navy men in the
Hawaiian area only one could qualify as a candidate for the
team. Norman resolved to be that man! This despite the fact
he excelled only as a horseman, while the Pentathlon embraces
shooting, fencing, swimming and running, as well as riding.
Norman had never fired a pistol, had never seen an épée, but he
could run and swim, although he was outstanding in neither. The
Hawaiian competition, preliminary to later trials in the United
States, was to embrace only running, swimming and shooting.
Norman's determination to win was as great if not greater than
mine had ever been. And win he did!

Norman was promptly shipped back to San Diego in June (I
was not there yet) and started intensive pistol-shooting practice
at the Camp Elliott Marine Corps range. Later that month he
was sent to Camp Lejeune, North Carolina, where he won the
All-Navy Triathlon (shooting, swimming and running) championship. Ahead lay the inter-service championships and now
the competition would be even sterner. However, Norman

wasn't daunted and he survived the elimination, which narrowed the contenders to fifteen, who were taken to Fort Belvoir,
Virginia.

Now, under Coach Jack Diamond, who had been the riding
and fencing instructor at West Point, Norman was introduced
to the épée, and, of course, riding was added. He was on a
dawn-to-dark schedule and he developed a phenomenal appetite
—a sample breakfast consisted of a dozen eggs and a huge piece
of ham. Oddly enough, he went from twelve stone down to ten.
'Everyone,' he said, 'lost weight.'

Meanwhile, I was returning from London with Nell Hopman
and I had written and asked Norman to meet me in New York.
Then we found a flight that would take us straight through to
Chicago, where I was to play in the United States National
Clay Court championships. I wrote Norman of the change in
plans, but he didn't receive the letter in time.

So Norman stood alone, waiting in vain at the New York
airport, and to make matters worse a reporter recognized him
and asked if he were meeting me. Norman nodded, and the
reporter sharpened his pencil for an interview on love and tennis.
But the plane landed without me. 'Did she stand you up?' the
reporter asked. 'I suppose so,' Norman replied. So the reporter
had a story—a broken romance—and it made the New York
papers.

I, of course, waited forlornly for Norman at the Chicago airport, certain I was the one who had been stood up. Still angry,
I called him in Virginia a day or two later, but I should never
have lifted the phone out of its cradle—we managed to get
farther apart than ever.

Heartsick and desolate, I returned to San Diego on July 19th,
and my smile for the reporters and photographers on that bleak,
misty morning was forced and fleeting. Conversation, it had
been said, is a means of concealing thought, and it was never
more so for me on that morning.

However, I was back with my mother and Aunt Gertrude
again, and Colonel Merryboy was waiting for me, so that took

up some of the emotional slack. I arranged to ride the next day with Mimi Stieler, a friend of mine, and Linda Thornton, her house guest from the East.

The ride started out pleasantly enough. I was in the lead, going slowly over a narrow trail on the shoulder of a road. Ahead, about a city square away, was a blind curve. It was then I heard a low rumbling noise. I saw a cement-mixer truck turn the corner swiftly, coming towards us. All three horses became nervous as the truck continued towards us without slackening speed.

We all waved and shouted to the driver in an effort to get him to slow down or stop, but he did neither. He set his course in the centre of the road. Mimi's horse, on the opposite side of the road from me, acted up. The driver swerved the truck towards me. As he started to thunder by, Colonel Merryboy wheeled. I remember the sharp sensation of stinging pain. I must have been knocked off balance, because I fell after my horse veered and ran down the centre of the road.

I remember looking at the white line dividing the road . . . of feeling my hands sting. I thought this ridiculous . . . I've skinned myself. As I started to rise, my right leg buckled. I managed to hop on my left leg to the side of the road, where I sat down. It was then I noticed blood had seeped through the leg of my riding togs, but I did not associate the sharp stinging sensation when the truck passed with the blood on my leg. Then I rolled up my trouser leg and saw my leg slashed to the bone, the flesh lying open. I screamed, started to cry, then I looked up. Colonel Merryboy had returned and stood beside me looking down. He wasn't even scratched.

Then the hand of fate, coincidence, call it what you will, reached out to me. A trained nurse, on an outing with her children, passed by, stopped her car and came to my aid. Fortunately she had a clean diaper in the car and she used this quickly to stanch the flow of blood.

Now as a crowd began to gather, I went into shock, with moments of hysteria and moments of complete calm as I waited for the ambulance. 'My tennis . . . my tennis . . . I'll never be able to play again,' I thought hysterically. Then, calmly, there came the clear knowledge that this meant the end of my tennis career. Weeping, I fought the thought back to the dark corners of my mind.

Finally the ambulance arrived and I was lifted up in a stretcher. I felt excruciating pain—something I have never experienced before or since. Bob Rice, the riding master, had hurried to the scene of the accident and rode with me in the ambulance. A young interne, his lips trembling slightly, was also at my side. 'Miss Connolly,' he said, 'you may bite my hand if it will help.'

His shocked expression momentarily broke the pain for me. I was sure this was his first case and he was more frightened than I, and I laughed : 'I'll hold your hand, but I won't bite it.'

Then began the strange hospital days—a series of pictures jumbled together, some painfully clear, others blurred, the timing uneven. Doctors, nurses, my mother, and several friends were there to meet me. I hadn't wanted to see Mom; I thought she'd faint, but she bore up, as always.

Nelson and Sophie Fisher, always steadfast friends, had reached the hospital almost before the ambulance. It was Sophie, who could not mask her grave expression of concern or stem an involuntary 'Oh, my God !' when she saw my leg, who made me fear again my days of glory on the courts lay behind.

I was in the operating room for four hours. Later, a plastic surgeon examined me, but withheld his opinion until later of the advisability of further surgery. All my right leg and calf muscles had been severed, the fibula bone broken, and, of course, a lot of skin on my leg had been ripped away. For three days and nights I was under heavy sedation, getting all types of shots every fifteen minutes. One nurse commented later I was the politest patient she ever had, always rolling over obediently for each shot and never forgetting to say : 'Thank you.'

After about four days my mind became clear, and I was suddenly aware my room was completely banked with flowers.

More than 500 wires, cables and letters were stacked up. Doris Hart, Nell Hopman and Vic Seixas were among the first three who sent wires.

On the fifth day there was a Press conference. I wanted none, but my doctor, Bruce Kimball, asked me to please talk briefly to the reporters as he wanted to get out from under a steady barrage of questions. Nelson Fisher acted as a buffer for me with the Press and everyone was extremely kind.

There is, I think, a silver lining to many tragedies, and for me there were threads which woven together gave life a new meaning, a new purpose. Part of this pattern unfolded one afternoon when the nurse announced a visitor, a Mr. Connolly.

A well-set-up man, with short grey hair, wearing a neat brown suit, came into the room. My mind raced back to the Pacific Southwest Tournament. This was the pleasant stranger, who had asked about my mother, who seemed, somehow, vaguely familiar. Now I knew! We looked at each other for a moment, then I was in my father's arms. Only because of my accident had he stepped across the chasm of years. It was a joyous reunion, the beginning of a new and wonderful relationship.

On the ninth day I started my come-back with a fifteen-minute whirl on crutches. I was utterly exhausted. Ironic? Only two weeks before I could race for hours on the courts . . . fleet, flashy, with what had been described as the best footwork in tennis.

So I was brought home, the letters and wires kept coming, but nothing from Norman. Finally he called. He hadn't seen any newspapers, hadn't heard the radio and learned the news casually from a chance acquaintance. He wanted to fly back to San Diego at once, but no Navy policy existed for a situation such as this. Norman had no written orders, merely verbal ones, and so, armed with a copy of *Life* magazine, with a picture story of our engagement, he laid siege to the Pentagon. Final clearance for his flight had to come from the Secretary of the Navy!

Norman arrived, but our romance didn't have a chance. I

was spent emotionally, worried about our engagement, the memory of past quarrels still fresh, and I built a high wall between us. We decided to break our engagement and I returned his ring, but we agreed to tell no one except our families. Norman thought we should wait, perhaps things might work themselves out, but I saw no hope. . . .

Here is Norman's story, which, by the way, has never been told fully, although the high-lights of it received world-wide coverage. He returned to Virginia and plunged back into training. The competition narrowed down to six men, who left on September 1st for Berlin. There the squad was pared to three men and an alternate, and this marked the first time in history two Navy men made the team—Norman and Ensign Bill Andre. The big competition was to be held in Budapest, with twelve nations entered in the finals.

Norman's first view of life behind the Iron Curtain was rather humorous. A small Russian soldier, armed with a machine-gun almost larger than he was, chased a little boy who appeared to be teasing him. In the pursuit, the soldier took a comic tumble. Then, with an expression of chagrin, he looked up and saw a two-car party, with the team and the United States military attaché, waiting patiently to pass the first Hungarian check point. The second check point had nothing in common with the first one. Here everything was strictly business. Towers bristled with machine guns. The fields were ploughed and mined; two barbed-wire fences loomed menacingly. The guards were formally polite and efficient.

Norman and the team, with the athletes from the other nations, stayed at the Red Star Hotel in Budapest, which overlooked the Danube. The plush Red carpet was rolled out and never taken up. Facilities and service were excellent; each team was given a training schedule, interpreters, transportation and drivers. Orders from the Kremlin must have been to 'Win Friends and Influence People.' There was never, according to Norman, anything resembling an 'incident' or any suggestion that 'American capitalists' were not nice people.

'We called our driver "Smiley," ' Norman told me, 'for the obvious reason that his face reflected no expression whatsoever. The Hungarian style of driving is to press down on the accelerator and the horn at the same time. We were in a cavalcade of twenty-four cars, bound for the mayor's party, and you could have heard the honking for miles.'

Norman was seated at a table with a Red colonel and his wife, who looked like a movie star. 'I had never seen as much food, or in such variety, in my life,' he said. The colonel, who spoke English, gave Norman a rose-coloured version of Hungary, with each bit of propaganda punctuated by a dazzling smile from the colonel's wife. 'I enjoyed it,' Norman said, 'and it was certainly a bang-up performance, but I wasn't sure it had too much in common with reality.'

The riding competition was scheduled for a Sunday, and each team was permitted to walk the course the day before and plan strategy. No one was allowed to ride over the course in advance, and the actual competition would be based upon time, as the riders would go individually. There were twenty-eight jumps—all the variety possible—with logs, steps, picket and stone fences and water jumps. On the unnumbered jumps there was a choice of two the rider could make.

'The Hungarians,' Norman told me, 'are great sports enthusiasts and also fine athletes. Although the course was forty-five miles out of town and no public transportation, a crowd of six thousand had assembled.'

There was a draw for mounts and Norman's horse was a small, powerfully made jet-black stallion, a bold jumper, and one of the best horses Norman had ever ridden. All of the jumpers, incidentally, were good. It was decided Norman should be the last man to ride on the United States team, and he felt confident, after giving his horse a brief trial. Here he would be competing in a sport where he excelled.

For twenty-four jumps Norman and the black stallion captured the imagination of the Hungarian crowd, many of whom had watches and clocked the time. Approaching the twenty-fifth jump, an excited spectator looked up from his watch and cried: 'You're first!' This jump was a pyramid of logs. 'We passed through a clump of trees with low overhanging branches,' Norman said. 'I was low, but as we approached the jump, my horse flattened out a bit, and when he leaped he miscalculated, making his jump too soon. He hit the top of the logs, fell and slid. I was used to spills; I'd never been hurt in a fall, and I thought this one would be no different than dozens of others. I held on to the reins, but as we slid along the horse's head hit my shoulder and shattered it.'

Norman, now in intense pain, remounted and took the black stallion over the last three jumps without a fault! It was really a feat, because the horse, although not injured, wanted to turn left and go back to the stables. Norman had a hard time trying to keep him straight. The spill, sad to relate, disqualified the American team (the Hungarian team won).

Doctors and nurses were at the finish line to meet Norman and he was promptly given a drink of whisky and a hypodermic injection to ease the pain. There was a slight language mix-up at this point, because Norm, in his mental fog, insisted his mount get a shot of whisky, too, and the doctors couldn't quite understand this equine therapy. A tiny ambulance rolled up to the finish and Norman refused to get in it; he wanted 'Smiley' or nothing. The Hungarians promptly produced 'Smiley,' and so Norman, with a doctor, was driven to the sports hospital, where athletes are the only patients.

Now, if you will permit a brief switch, let's go back momentarily to San Diego. By this time I had recovered and was writing a column for the *San Diego Union*. One of the editors handed me a news dispatch under a Budapest dateline and I read of Norman's accident. I had difficulty finishing the story. I was stunned and sick. I phoned Mom, asked her to come and get me. At home, I got off a cable, then started writing a letter to Norman. I was crying, the letter was incoherent. I knew I loved him, wanted him, and couldn't do without him. I almost tore up the letter, but finally I mailed it.

Norman's reply, composed while he was under sedation, was just as incoherent as mine. It was written in graph-like waves; it took me an hour and a half to decipher it, but he loved me! It took two serious accidents to bring us close again, but now we started writing regularly, and I was sure no hurdle lay ahead which we couldn't clear together.

In the Budapest hospital, Norman was a curiosity—the first American patient—and something of a celebrity. The story of his accident received world-wide newspaper and magazine coverage; it was the first time anyone had ever finished the course with a shattered shoulder. Furthermore, the United States Minister and the military attaché had come to visit Norman in the hospital, carrying stacks of magazines and a big supply of cigarettes and chocolates. Such attention was so unusual that it set Norman off as a patient apart.

'It turned out to be an amazing experience,' Norman said. 'I had a Hungarian room-mate who spoke English, a highly educated man, and it didn't take him long to discover I was just an average twenty-three-year-old American boy, not an intelligence officer, and in no way connected with an attempt to spread sweetness-and-light propaganda about the United States. [Obviously, Norman was not a 'plant.']

'This,' Norman continued, 'put me in an unusual position. The Hungarians trooped into our room at all hours. I had magazines, cigarettes and chocolates to share with everyone. The Hungarians believed that I alone was in a position to tell the truth about my country. They had been fed a rich and heavy propaganda diet and this excess had the effect of making them uncertain what to believe about the United States. It also made me weigh my words carefully, trying to tell them the truth as I knew it without colouring what I said.'

Norman was under a friendly third degree at all times. Sample questions:

'Why was Charlie Chaplin kicked out of the United States?'
'What about armed labour uprisings in Detroit?'
'Would America attack Russia?'

'Did Norman own a car? How much did it cost?'

The questions, Norman said, were endless, but I am certain the United States never had a younger 'ambassador' than Norman or one who was more trusted. All the patients became eager to visit America, and I suppose I should tell you Norman has a natural flair for selling.

After a conference of the medical staff, the decision to operate was left to Norman. There was a good chance surgery would make Norman's arms equal in length. There also was the possibility that it might fail. In time, the shoulder would knit well, but his left arm would be fractionally shorter. Norman decided against an operation; he wanted the advice of the surgeons in Berlin. However, the American doctors in Berlin agreed completely with the Budapest opinion, and Norman was not operated on and his shoulder healed perfectly.

In San Diego I was embarking upon the hardest struggle of my life.

CHAPTER FOURTEEN

I THINK I know what 'The Long Road Back' really means, whether it be a defeated army, fighting to regain lost ground, a fighter arising from the canvas to face crushing blows, or anyone making a great struggle against titanic odds. If spirit alone, determination alone, or struggle alone could have won my goal, I still would be the girl with the Golden Racket.

Picking up a marble with my toes became for me the most important thing in the world. I picked up a million, give or take a few. Nothing was overlooked in my surging drive to regain the high ground of tennis. I had exercises, the whirlpool treatment. I would have done anything and everything to reach the top again. I was placed in a half-cast, as the doctor feared if he put me in a walking cast I might try to gallop at once. After three or four weeks, I walked a little, the stretch in my leg began to return slowly and I abandoned crutches.

The accident occurred on July 20th and by September I ventured cautiously on the tennis court. I stood in one position, hit a few balls, anxious to keep my timing sharp, and rallying just long enough to satisfy myself I still had the touch. I did this twice a week, but there was absolutely no running. I may have been eager, but I was cautious, too. Nothing was going to interfere with my come-back. The future was clearly mapped : I would defend my titles at Wimbledon and Forest Hills in 1955, then turn professional in 1956.

My doctor gave me permission to take up ballet, and for me this was a dedicated undertaking, embarked upon with the intensity a Russian ballerina might show. Joanne Thornbrooke, my instructress, saw I was no casual pupil, and she treated me as if I were working towards a great career on the stage. For two months I worked tirelessly on the bars, stretching, lifting, bending—anything to strengthen my muscles.

Suddenly a danger sign appeared. Whenever I put strenuous pressure on my right leg, the area under the scar would turn blue and there would be an accompanying temperature change as this part of my leg would become colder. I began developing terrible leg cramps. This, at first, was considered just a part of the healing process.

The months sped along and this peculiar condition did not improve. By January 1955 the malignant but stifled suspicion in the back of my mind—I would never play championship tennis again—grew now like a gathering black cloud. I simply could not start and stop quickly without shooting pains in my leg.

Defeat, as I told you, had been my shadow since the first days on the courts, but as I rose to the top, won all my titles, I thought perhaps my career might go on for years. I could imagine facing a young girl, who would have every stroke I possessed, but she would back her bid with youth. Under this assault I would tire and crumble just as other girls had done against me. This was the end I saw—the old champion bowing before the young challenger.

But the setting at the beautiful La Jolla Beach and Tennis Club under a cloudless February sky was like nothing I had imagined for my swan song. I had the strokes, perfect and deadly weapons, and I was getting the 'big serve'—the one shot I lacked. Les Stoefen, the pro, tall, smiling and considerate, but a formidable foe, stood across the court. No one else was there, no crowds, no photographers, no journalists with dead-lines to meet, yet Stoefen, for me, was every Wimbledon foe rolled into one and I resolved to fight him each step of the way. We began playing, and, before a few points were won and lost, he executed a tricky drop shot. I determined to return it. I remember pushing off fast on my right leg, but a terrible shoot-ing pain stopped me in my tracks. I still kept trying, but now I was going for nothing wide, made no swooping rushes for short shots.

'What's wrong, Maureen?' Les kept asking.

I gritted my teeth, didn't reply, but kept on trying, until finally I admitted what I must have known in my heart for so long. 'Les, I just know I can't play any more.'

And thus, I alone, of all the world's women tennis champions, was through at twenty, holder of every major crown in the world. Was this a solace for bitterness? The cups, the clippings, the memories? No, only my marriage brought me happiness, erased bitterness, cancelled out the area of 'what might have been,' substituted tranquillity, the ability to look backwards with dispassion, to look ahead with confidence, to change direction.

Through the period of my futile come-back, marked by one crying jag after another, Norman, who had returned from Europe, stood by me, lending me his courage and strength. Now, as I told him about my match with Les Stoefen, he listened quietly, then took command. He told me I must quit trying, that he would not allow me to torture myself. We would get married. He held me in his arms, my turbulent emotions drained away, and I felt peace and tranquillity even though I knew my days of glory on the court lay behind, never to be recaptured.

Announcement of my retirement from tennis, plus the news of my coming wedding, was carried throughout the world by the Press wire services. Foolishly I did not tell the truth. I said I had lost interest in tennis. I wanted no sympathy for a come-back that failed. Neither did I want anyone to believe I was marrying Norman because I could no longer play championship tennis. Telling the simple truth would have been far better.

I would be a June bride! This would be a big church wedding and there were a million details. Teddy Tinling cabled me from London, reminding me of his promise to make my wedding gown. Teddy piled one thrill on top of another when he sent me another cable saying he had arranged for Aage Thaarup, the Queen's milliner, to fashion my head-dress. I thought surely I was the luckiest girl in the world.

Teddy air-expressed five designs and a lot of material for my wedding dress. Three designs were incorporated in the one I chose. The material was scalloped lace; the design a princess style, with a sweetheart neck, long sleeves—finger-tip length— with a short train under a large satin slip, with the lace so designed it would show at intervals around the bottom of the skirt. The lace would separate, and the satin slip, designed like a rose petal, would be revealed. Under the slip I wore a beautiful hoop skirt of chiffon decorated with lilies of the valley. Everything was hand-sewn and exquisite. Although I was an American girl, Teddy Tinling couldn't have created anything more beautiful had I been English Royalty.

The head-dress (and may I make a curtsy to the Queen's taste in milliners) was small, petal-shaped and decorated with orange blossoms. It had an illusion veil, which was waist-length, covered my face, but could be lifted for the ceremony.

The wedding rehearsals were nightmarish, and if it is the traditional role of the bride to be nervous I qualified completely. The day of the wedding we were besieged by reporters, news-reel cameramen and photographers. But Norman remained calm, steady—truly the Rock of Gibraltar.

Then, the wedding. The church was decorated with Maureen Connolly dahlias, named for me and grown by Mrs. Paul Comstock. They were beautiful. At last, I walked down the aisle, holding on to Norman's arm—jittery as a yearling colt. Suddenly I felt Norman's arm shake. He, too, was nervous! Suddenly the situation became so ironic I gave a tiny laugh and became completely at ease. Bishop Buddy, looking at Norman, said in a soft, kindly voice: 'You are doing fine. Steady now.' It was Norman, not I, who needed temporal support in the church. The Bishop deviated from the usual marriage ceremony by giving a short talk about Norman and me as an ideal young couple—both accomplished athletes, each a credit to the world of sport. It was not planned; it flowed from his heart, and as I look back now it almost seems as if he were giving away his own little girl, who had looked to him as a father for guidance and comfort.

We went to Warner's Hot Springs in San Diego County for our honeymoon—a beautiful place set among large trees, with natural hot sulphur springs. We had each other and we were completely happy with this simple and idyllic honeymoon.

But the telephone rang. London was calling. The London *Daily Mail* wanted me to cover Wimbledon for them. I promptly said: 'No.' I was on my honeymoon and nothing could separate me from Norman. Then the phone rang again. The *Daily Mail* was willing to pay Norman's travel expenses as well as mine. So our honeymoon became an extended tour— London, the French Riviera, Rome, Naples, Venice, Switzerland and Paris.

We returned home on the *Queen Mary* and she will remain for ever my favourite ship. We met Richard Burton, the famous English actor, and his wife, and the meeting developed into a warm friendship and we enjoyed the Burtons tremendously on the voyage home.

It might be presumed by some that I turned with great eagerness to legal redress. This is not true. I had never been inside a courtroom. I held the quaint belief that courts were for the guilty alone, and I had a horror of experiencing any action that might involve me. It was after long deliberation and with considerable hesitancy that I filed a damage action against the firm which owned the concrete-mixer truck. I believed in the truth of my cause, but there could be no financial reward which would erase the dark nightmare of the accident and put me back again on the centre court.

Melvin H. Belli, of San Francisco, who is one of America's finest personal injury lawyers, took my case at the suggestion of mutual friends. In this action he was associated with John Butler, former mayor of San Diego. Whenever Belli makes a court appearance, I am told, dozens of young lawyers attend to observe his legal technique. I expected an elderly, austere barrister, one who might fit a wig naturally, so I was not prepared for the smiling, boyish and friendly man in his forties who was to plead my cause. Mel is different from any attorney I ever met, but he has power, a brilliant mind, a low, nicely modulated voice, but above all else a compelling sincerity.

With me, Belli had a distinct handicap. I was an extremely poor witness; I was afraid; the courtroom became the centre court at Wimbledon, but now I held no racket. I had to talk, and my machine-gun delivery was no asset because it became difficult for judge and jury to understand what I had to say. One factor, I believe, weighed in my favour. I always have tried to be honest. When the opposing attorney questioned my story, I became enraged, or, at least, I seethed inside. This was the first time in my life my honesty had been questioned and the question was raised in public. I think both judge and jury saw my eyes flash with anger as I looked or tried to stare down my questioner, giving my answers with no hesitancy.

Belli relied heavily upon expert medical testimony—a field where he excels. He not only understands anatomy as well as a surgeon, but he has the ability, which many doctors lack, of being able to put things simply, explain graphically in non-technical language which anyone can understand.

Before we went to court, Belli had exhaustive examinations made of my leg and I was taken to plastic surgeons in both San Diego and Los Angeles. There was no dissent in the opinion that the horrid scar and dent in my leg could never be removed by surgery. During the trial, we were fortunate to have the testimony of Dr. Tom O'Connell, one of America's foremost vascular experts. Vascular tests showed the main artery in my right leg had been permanently impaired. The testimony of Dr. Paul Shea, who with Dr. O'Connell heads the physical therapy department at Mercy Hospital, was heightened by the fact that he played tennis, had played against me, and understood the great divide between social and championship tennis.

Jack Kramer, former world's tennis champion, and now the world's leading promoter of professional tennis, testified for me, saying, in his opinion, I could have earned about $150,000 in two years as a pro. I, of course, had planned joining Kramer's entourage. Tom Harmon, one of America's all-time great football players, and now a television and radio sports commentator, likewise testified on my behalf.

The jury returned a judgment of $95,000—the highest in the history of San Diego County. As this is written, the case is under appeal.

Strangely enough, for me, there was a sad aftermath. My popularity nose-dived in my own home town. Many people could not understand why I should have won an award in court. I had not been crippled, I wore no crutches, carried no cane, and, on the surface, at least, I appeared quite normal. But the glory of championship tennis was gone, the chance for world-wide pro tours was lost, and never would I achieve the real zenith of my game.

'What was she doing on a horse?' was the comment of some. Yet, only the year before, the people of San Diego had given me a horse. Such is irony and such is the fleeting warmth of popularity.

Norman and I settled down in a small house in Mission Valley, which has a corral where I keep Colonel Merryboy. I became a tennis instructor, while Norman, out of the Navy, returned to college.

My life has become completely different, but wonderful, too. I no longer know the grinding pressure of the centre court, I shall for ever be a stranger to the realm I ruled.

I had given up my kingdom for a horse.

PART TWO

LOOKING BACK

CHAPTER FIFTEEN

THIS IS MY PARIS-ROME-BERLIN EXPRESS, with a short side-trip to Ireland. The world was my oyster, a Golden Racket my passport, and I wanted to see everything, play everywhere, but most of all I wanted history to come alive for me, and it did. I made two tours in 1953 and 1954, then returned to England, Italy, and France on my honeymoon the next year. I'll try to pack in the high-lights for you, but there's more sightseeing than tennis.

Perry T. Jones, secretary of the Southern California Tennis Association, sat down with me at luncheon at the Hotel del Coronado to arrange the tour.

'Where would you like to go, Maureen?' he asked.

'Everywhere!' I fired back.

He threw up his hands in alarm. Slowly, patiently, he explained the 'everywhere' tour would be much too much, that I would play in too many tournaments, that I would become over-tennised and I would reach Wimbledon, not at a peak, but at the depths of my game.

I was ready for Jones. I told him I had learned to pace myself, that Harry Hopman was coming to Europe and I'd have the advantage of his splendid coaching before Wimbledon and that would put me on edge and I would be at my best for the 'big one.'

Jones, of course, was right. No tour such as I planned belongs in a champion's schedule. A few well-spaced tournaments, intensive practice, then Wimbledon, would have been the best tennis medicine. But I wasn't having any.

'Maureen's young,' Jones told a friend later. 'She wants to see the world, and I suppose I shouldn't blame her for that. After all, she's the world's champion.' (The champion in Jones's scheme of things deserved special treatment.)

Nell Hopman was to be our chaperone and Julie Sampson would make the trip with me. First stop Rome. I, of course, fell in love with Italy, just as I fell in love with every place we went. Tennis now was secondary to sightseeing, and on my European and Continental tours I was more a tourist with a camera than a girl with a devastating racket.

Rome's Fore de Italico, built by Mussolini for the Italian youth, was the most lavish sports centre I had ever seen. There were stadiums for tennis, swimming and rugby, all fashioned out of marble. Statues of heroic proportions depicting legendary Roman athletes surrounded the stadia, and the tennis stadium truly was unique. There were six outside courts and one stadium court. To reach the stadium court, it was necessary to go through a block-long, dimly lit tunnel and the experience gave one the feeling of a Christian being sent out as lion fodder.

Time, to the Italians, is less than the essence; no one, it seemed, appeared in the stadium court before two or three in the afternoon. Then, too, the scheduling of matches was a bit haphazard. Doris Hart, one of the world's finest players, found herself slated to play at nine o'clock in the morning. Later in the dressing-room she told me: 'We had a great audience—all those dead-tired statues.' Not a soul had shown up to see her play an Italian girl. Doris won that match in a hurry, love and love.

There is nothing quite like that stadium court. There are no backdrops, just a vast and tremendous expanse. All players, consciously or unconsciously, use the backdrops as a measuring gauge, but here there was much more wide-open space than Wimbledon, although the pressure, of course, was not the same. As a prelude, the cars assigned to take us to the stadium never arrived on time, but we solved that by ordering them an hour earlier. The playing surface is of fine reddish clay and it's difficult at first to get one's touch and the tendency is to over-hit. At least, it was for me. Doris beat me in the 1953 finals in three sets and she deserved the triumph, but the loss, for me, was not heartbreaking.

Now, the Roman tour. We visited St. Sebastian's catacombs, with a priest for a guide. The Aussie team was with us and Mervyn Rose managed his own special brand of humour whenever he could bring it into play. There were about fifteen of us walking in single file through the passage, lit only by guttering candles, set in wall niches. The candles didn't gutter long. Rose blew them out in passing, and I, at the end of the line, was plunged into total darkness. An unladylike shriek brought light. We saw the rooms where the Christian martyrs had died and there was the room where St. Peter had come to meditate before he was crucified.

One of my most memorable Roman experiences was a visit to St. Peter's Cathedral, which for beauty and majesty is without comparison in the world. Fortunately, a couple from Chicago recognized me, and asked if Nell and I would like to accompany them. This was a great stroke of fortune, because their son was in the Roman priesthood and he had arranged for Monsignor Hugh O'Flaherty, a Vatican authority and author, to conduct a special tour. Monsignor O'Flaherty was a charming man with keen intelligence and wit, and he was explaining things he loved and had made his life's work. There is only one oil painting in the cathedral, but there are the most beautiful mosaics I have ever seen and they decorate the walls of the many altars.

Then we were taken to the workshop where the mosaics were made, and here was an inspiring sight. Deaf mutes, working from sketches or paintings, created the mosaics, which were made much larger than the originals from which they worked. I have never seen men more possessed with love of their work or endowed with the ability to create such beautiful works of art. I almost stepped on an angel's wings as I wandered trance-like about the workshop. A quick restraining hand saved me.

I, of course, am no authority on precious stones, but I can still remember vividly the glittering collection of Papal jewels and robes, which are kept in glass cases in a special room. The jewels were large and incredibly beautiful and the robes brought to mind at once the pomp and pageantry of the Holy Roman Church. It seemed to me, however, that such fabulous gems should be kept behind the doors of a massive vault, so I asked Monsignor O'Flaherty why they were not guarded more closely. He explained that only once had there been attempted theft. The thief had stolen several million dollars' worth of the jewels, but he was caught before he could leave the Vatican grounds.

Perhaps you have seen the Sistine Chapel, but I never had, and I was overwhelmed by the two paintings by Michelangelo, which took years to finish. Monsignor O'Flaherty had the chapel opened specially for us and we drank in the beauty as if it were the rarest wine in the world. The story of the Creation is painted on the ceiling and the Last Judgment is on the front wall. Monsignor O'Flaherty told us a fascinating story about the Last Judgment. Originally, Michelangelo painted the figures nude. However, the monsignor who was in charge of the project objected and refused to permit them to remain undraped. Michelangelo, furious, went to the Pope, who backed up the monsignor and the artist was forced to clothe the figures. But the painter had revenge. Monsignor O'Flaherty showed us the painting of a man, with a snake winding around his body, in the lower right-hand corner. This depicted Satan, but the face of Satan was the face of the monsignor whom Michelangelo hated!

We saw the Papal chapel where the Pope comes to pray and meditate. It is here the Catholic hierarchy meets to select a new Pope. The secret votes are burned in a chimney-like affair, but when the selection is made there is a special signal of this great event for the multitudes who wait outside. They can see a whitish smoke emerge from the chimney, and this becomes an occasion for rejoicing and prayer.

Our guide for the Coliseum of Rome was the same one that General Eisenhower had used, and he had a photograph of himself with the General to prove his point. I am not sure, however, that Eisenhower got a correct briefing on Coliseum history. This guide accentuated the plight of the Christians and the ferocity of the lions, but on my second trip to the Coliseum we had another guide with a totally different version. Happily, Eisenhower is a keen student of history and he may have known more than either guide about the subject at hand. I succeeded only in becoming confused, although I enjoyed every minute of it and managed to find, not a lion, but a starving kitten on the Coliseum floor. I at once decided to take her on tour; Nell objected, but I was able to find the kitten a rich Roman home.

Pompeii, of course, is fascinating. I did not know the eruption of Mount Vesuvius had been triggered by the eruption of a smaller volcano which parallels it. We saw two figures of men, preserved by the molten lava, both studies in horror and fear. One man died shielding his face, the other perished cringing from the engulfing tide of lava. Nothing, I think, reflects more clearly the horror and tragedy of the event. We also saw the fabled Pompeii red—a colour that has never been duplicated. It is deep, soft and beautiful.

Florence, Milan, Venice, Naples—we visited them all—and there is a special beauty and charm in each. The churches of Italy, the art galleries and the craftsmanship are special things apart in my memory. I could not understand, however, why more effort is not made to preserve the ruins, which continue to deteriorate, and I found it hard to adjust to the cliff-like drop between wealth and extreme poverty.

My trips to Germany were like my other travel adventures, thrilling and beautiful, and if I may offer a travel tip, by virtue of my battle-scarred suitcases, here it is: go while you're young, don't put it off until age draws its mists of indifference and cynicism over your eyes. A third-class ticket at twenty is far better than a de luxe trip at fifty.

Primarily, my purpose (the official reason) was to play exhibitions for the U.S. Armed Forces, but really I came to see Germany, and I did. The tennis was strictly incidental. I had fun playing exhibitions. The tournaments were not taxing, because Germany has not regained its pre-war status on the courts. The girls are good, but hardly in the same bracket with the top American players, and the boys do not compare to the Aussie players.

I fell in love with two horses (naturally), but these were statues of dapple-grey stallions—one rearing, the other in a regal pose. We were visiting a Munich glass-works and china factory and I admired both of these unusual works of art. They were given to me and now they occupy a special place in our home. I have tried many times to curb my natural enthusiasm for things I like, because it often places one in the embarrassing position of having them offered to you are gifts. Such admiration is a cue for some hosts to bestow a gift, and there can be no gracious refusal. I once admired a savage-looking stuffed mountain lion in the official palace of the governor of a Mexican state. He promptly gave it to me, and when I demurred his aide explained the governor would be highly offended if I refused the present. (It's a good thing I didn't admire an Indian elephant.)

Heidelberg, I think, is one of the world's most beautiful and unusual cities, with the storybook-like houses set on the hillsides overlooking the Rhine. We visited a famous inn, sipped delicious beer, and I closed my eyes and the 'Drinking Song' came back to me, because it was here Sigmund Romberg composed it for *The Student Prince*. We saw some of Germany's most famous duelling grounds, where the badge of the duelling fraternity was the scarred cheek. Although duelling, of course, is illegal now, I was shocked to see several handsome German boys with fresh sabre cuts marring their cheeks.

The University of Heidelberg is famous for its scholars, but I didn't know punishment could have been as severe as it was many years ago for lack of scholastic brilliance. We were taken to the cellars underneath the university and here were bare cubicles where students were once isolated and put on a bread-and-water diet.

Berlin, at least the western sector, had been largely rebuilt, with the accent on modern structure. We didn't visit the eastern sector, although the Mervyn Rose brand of humour became

ABOVE LEFT *Norman's fall at Budapest*
RIGHT *The winner's twirl 1952*
BELOW *In Australia with Harry Hopman and Jack Purtel*

*'Little Mo' at seventeen in action against Britain's
Mrs I. Rinkel-Quartier during the Britain v. United
States Wightman Cup team at Wimbledon 1952*

operative at the Brandenburg Gate. It was less than a hit with
the Soviets. Mervyn and I took pictures of each other at the
war memorial statue which borders the Soviet zone. Mervyn
saw some Russian soldiers near by, off duty and apparently
enjoying themselves. Mervyn, as a joke, pointed his camera at
one soldier, who reacted violently, first shaking his fist, then
bringing up his gun. Mervyn and I established new Berlin track
records in our retreat.

Ireland, the home of my ancestors, is beautiful, green and
drenched with hospitality, liquid and otherwise. I was there
twice, enjoying the sights more than the tennis, but each visit
was brief, and the National Irish Stud Farm outside of Dublin
naturally frames my most vivid memories. Tulyar, the magnificent stallion, had been purchased from the Aga Khan, and this
caused tremendous excitement. Services to Tulyar were so in
demand that breeders drew lots and the lucky ones sent their
mares to his court.

It was at the stud farm I saw a fabulous Chinese tea-garden
symbolic of life and death, with each facet of the landscaping
part of the story. Entrance to the garden was through a cave of
darkness, and one came, like a baby from the womb, into the
brilliance of life's sunshine. There were paths—the path of life—
joined as the story of marriage unfolded. Babies, children,
separation, reconciliation, death, cremation and a final resting
place were depicted in this wondrous garden.

Our car ride through the curraghs, which are wide unfenced
fields, compared favourably with the suicidal tactics of the more
daring taxi-cab drivers in Rome, Paris and Tia Juana. Flocks
of sheep were the hazards in this pastoral setting, and we travelled a narrow and slippery lane at breakneck speed, narrowly
avoiding the reduction or total elimination of the four-footed
population.

The Irish wanted to produce a family tree for us, and my
first trip, made with my mother, produced a highly dubious
genealogy. It was claimed, at first, that Mom had two sons, plus
a daughter, and this, of course, was news to both of us. Then
5—FD

an Irish newspaper-man, intent upon making headlines, dredged up a female derelict, with a patch over one eye and an aura of Irish whiskey. She was to be introduced to us as Mom's long-lost aunt. The ceremony, if one may call it that, was to take place in Dublin on the afternoon of the finals. Mother simply refused to have any part of this hoax; she had no long-lost aunt, and she wasn't about to embrace one for the sake of newspaper circulation.

The Dublin tournament is great fun, with a round of official parties. Irish tennis is handicapped by rain, and although the grass courts are perfect the players don't get enough time to practise and the elements keep Ireland from having really championship tennis.

Paris in the springtime!

Now the time was getting nearer to Wimbledon, and, although I managed some sightseeing and shopping, the training became more rigorous, because the world's big tennis goal was looming ahead.

I imagine every girl loves Paris. I did. The shopping, of course, was disappointing, because my funds were limited and the prices high. But I did a lot of window shopping along the Champs-Elysées. I remember one experience. I had $60 for a dress, and I saw a cute navy-blue number, quite simple. The saleswoman told me it was $160 and I was properly shocked. 'My dear,' she said with true Parisian cynicism, 'there are many Americans who will be happy to pay the price.' Not I. However, I bought some lovely silks, as I had done in Italy, and Teddy Tinling made them up into stunning dresses for me.

We, of course, saw all the Paris sights, including the inevitable visit to the Folies Bergère, which I enjoyed. Ken Rosewall was sitting on the aisle beside me, and a dancing girl, scantily clad, came down the aisle, stopping to kiss the men. I heard an unmistakable roar a few rows behind me, looked and saw the Australian team trying to get my attention and pointing to Rosewall, who is naturally shy. I caught the cue, beckoned the dancing girl, and indicated Ken as an object of her affection.

Ken turned a true Pompeii red, but as the girl almost reached him she apparently got a signal from the stage. She smiled and said, 'Not thees time, *chéri*,' and returned to the ensemble. Ken's sigh of relief might have been a sigh he would make after winning a long, hard match.

Rex Hartwig wanted to go to the top of the Eiffel Tower, but his team-mates told him he couldn't make this trip until after he lost, because all that climbing would exhaust him, and there was no elevator. Of course, there is, and as we drove by one afternoon Rex saw it and demanded to go up at once. 'That's not permitted,' Rosewall told him, 'it's only for the infirm.' I hope by this time Rex has learned differently.

I loved the French food, the excellent seasoning and the superb sauces, but I didn't sample too much of this *haute cuisine*, nor was there much night life for me, because tennis was supposed to be my prime purpose. I remember one evening, however, at an official party, where I think I experienced the true Parisian gaiety. The music was gay, then sad, everyone appeared to be having a wonderful time and the food was excellent. Suddenly Mervyn took my hand, and started polishing it with a napkin. I had no idea why. Then Jean Borotra, one of tennis's great French musketeers, came up to our table, bowed in courtly fashion and kissed Nell's and Julie's hands. Mervyn got up, bowed to Jean, held my hand out, and said: 'Monsieur, this hand has been especially polished for the occasion.' Jean was baffled, but his kiss was deft.

My tennis, as Perry Jones was sure it would, suffered on this tour. The competition, for the most part, had been soft, and when one wins a string of easy matches there is a marked tendency to let down, stretch for a shot instead of step into it. My tennis, to say the least, lacked sparkle, and my forehand, a siege gun in my armament, had the fire-power of a toy cannon. I began practising with Fred Perry, who was in Paris and a bit alarmed about my game. He thought, and it was a natural conclusion, that if I concentrated on steadiness, my touch would come back. It didn't.

Harry Hopman came over at this point to join the Australian team, and he looked at me in a first-round match with complete despair. I at once went under the Hopman regimen, which is equivalent to two really tough sets of championship tennis. Hop was determined to have me in shape for Wimbledon.

On the way to the Roland Garros stadium is a beautiful drive through the Bois de Bologne district, with its paths, bridle trails and lakes. I had thrilled at this sight, but suddenly it became less enchanting. It was this sector Hop chose for our roadwork, and in one jaunt I managed to get lost and ran several extra miles out of my way. I, however, was not alone in need of conditioning. It was on this running expedition that I saw Ken Rosewall, far from Hop's watchful eye, sitting beside a tree, trying to get a moment's rest from this exacting routine.

Now I was starting to 'go for my shots,' and although my game had not reached the peak it would for Wimbledon, the touch was returning. Sometimes I think I played only as well as the particular occasion demanded. Nancy Chaffee Kiner always maintained I was far more dangerous when I was behind, and towards the end of my career this was the prime reason the other girls feared me. Nancy, of course, could be prejudiced in my favour.

Although my tennis improved, my match in the finals that year—1954—was not inspiring. I played against Jeanette Bucaille, winning in straight sets. She had a soft, tricky game and I show to better advantage, at least to the spectator, when I can cut loose my power game.

However, I would rather watch the French and Italian galleries in action than see the tennis. The spectator is volatile, the cheers are piercing, the groans agonizing and the gestures unbelievable.

Well, our express has chugged to a stop, but I can always close my eyes and have a front seat on this marvellous tour.

CHAPTER SIXTEEN

YOU ARE THE TENNIS AUDIENCE and to enjoy a championship match, to savour the strategy, understand the stress and
probe the play, it is necessary to penetrate deeper than just a
knowledge of the rules and a familiarity with the strokes. It is my
hope here to give you an 'inside look,' and, in passing, touch a
bit on 'gamesmanship' and perhaps offer a fashion note for
the girls.

England sees the world's best tennis, enjoys it the most, understands it the best and provides the finest 'audience.' The player,
like the actor, reacts to this stimulus by achieving a peak at
Wimbledon never attained anywhere else.

Now let's watch a mythical match and really enjoy it. We
should applaud good play after a point has been earned, but
never during the rally. Unfortunately, in America, players are
often distracted by the cries of enthusiastic spectators while play
is in progress. No matter how partisan a crowd might be,
applauding errors is poor form. Neither, by the way, is a freak
shot worthy of praise.

Keep your eyes open for the fine play, the tactics of the
game. A hard shot is not necessarily the best one, although it
draws the loudest applause.

Outright placements—the shots which are impossible to return—are the rare gems of tournament play. Only a shade
dimmer in lustre are the placements which force errors in the
attempted return. However, the prelude to the placement—
pulling one's opponent out of position, usually by wide or angle
shots—may be far more difficult than the execution of the actual
placement itself.

Few champions play two matches exactly alike, as attack and
defence must be varied to suit the situation. Change of pace is

a potent weapon. Watch for it and you will know what is going on in the mind of a player. For instance, a hard shot to the backhand, then an easy shot with top spin to the forehand, might earn a subtle point. Usually, a switch in tactics comes when a player is losing. A swift decision often is made to diversify the attack, soften the shots, use chops and cuts, substitute a tricky short game for a hard baseline offensive which hasn't been working.

The 'big serve' and the perfect ace always bring a cheer, but let's go a bit deeper here, and first weigh the number of aces against the number of double faults. The ace takes something out of a player; it is strictly a power serve and the player puts everything he or she has into the shot. Lew Hoad, who has tremendous strength plus powerful and supple wrists, is the only player I have ever seen who executes the ace effortlessly. Alice Marble once told me : 'Get your second serve in first.' This tactic has definite psychological advantage.

The best serves in the game, at least in my opinion, are those which break wide. One's opponent will go for them, but the return is difficult and a drain on stamina. The return often gives one a set-up, but now, instead of putting away this set-up for a sure point, let's consider strategy. My tactic here was to tire the foe, give her a return which she could make, but make only by running. Thus the initiative remained mine and I was trying to soften up my opponent for the second set. A fresh player will run for everything, but if you can keep the pressure on she will never get a 'second wind.'

It may sound far-fetched, but there is a definite similarity between a bull-fight and my favourite tennis tactics. I saw the incomparable Carlos Aruzza at the Plaza del Toros in Tia Juana once and was struck by the manner in which he handled the bull. First, he observed it closely in the preliminary phase of the fight. How did it hook its horns? Left or right? Did the bull charge straight? What sector of the ring did the bull consider its 'home' or, as the Mexicans say, the *quarentia*? Here the bull would be more dangerous. Aruzza watched each pass made by the other matadors, and when he faced the bull he knew its characteristics perfectly.

For Aruzza there was no quick kill. He strove for complete domination, a mastery over the bull, making it do whatever he wanted, and each pass was calculated to make the bull lower its head a bit, so, when the kill came, the sword would go in over the horns. Near the end, the bull was tired, almost hypnotized, and the kill, for me, was anti-climactic.

Now, with a tennis racket, not a cape, I hope to show you the comparison. My *quarentia* was the back-court. Here I felt an opponent could be vanquished because I was playing on my favourite battlefield. But the task would be easier if I had weakened my opponent, forced her to run continually, before I applied the full power of my game.

In order to achieve this, it was necessary for me to develop an all-round game, to attempt perfect deception and to master the drop shot and the lob. As I said, I favoured the wide-breaking serve, but I did not use this exclusively, because a defence could be set up against it—my opponent would know what to expect. I would mix this serve with a slice, which sent the ball into my foe, thus making her use a cramped shot in the return. Then perhaps I would serve a hard one down the line, and this might be an ace, although it lacked the classic speed of an ace. It fell within the category because one's opponent expected something else and was caught flatfooted.

Now let's consider deception. It is possible for one player to have a better game, stroke for stroke, than her foe, but still be vulnerable because deception is missing. Amateur boxing may offer the best example of lack of deception, and, by the same token, a public notice of intentions. A boxer—let's pick a clumsy one—drops his right shoulder, pulls his right arm back, and telegraphs his punch. Tennis players do this, too. If you watch closely, you know many times in advance what type of shot will be used and the direction the ball will take.

I practised hundreds of hours on the drop shot, and I believe I achieved deception. I came forward in exactly the same manner as if I were trying for a forehand drive. Yet, just before I hit, I would stop my racket, thus achieving the necessary soft, deft touch. Unless a spectator were unusually keen, he would consider this an easy shot. Believe me, it wasn't. In contrast, many other girls would get set in a certain way for the drop shot and I would know what to expect.

It is almost axiomatic that the extended left hand will point the direction of the ball, yet I tried to perfect two shots, both deceptive, which did not follow this rule. I think one of the really great shots is the backhand down the line, much harder to bring off than the backhand cross-court, which is much more natural. This down-the-line shot is tremendously difficult because it requires perfect timing, but it's invincible and a sure passing shot. In the first place, all tennis players move better to the left than to the right. More liberties are taken with the forehand than the backhand. One has to be set perfectly for the backhand. So, if you see this backhand down the line, well, you may be sure that countless hours of practice went into the shot.

In order to achieve deception, I would occasionally change the flight of my racket and put a forehand down my opponent's forehand court line, rather than to her backhand, where my left hand indicated it should travel. This, of course, is not good tennis, but it can be effective.

Now watch for the perfect lob, used as a strategic weapon and not a desperation shot. A nicely timed lob can throw an opponent's game out of gear momentarily; it is also a sound defensive shot, enabling one to get in position for the next shot, to regain the initiative.

The volley game is a thing apart; watch closely and you often can pick out the novice at the net from the seasoned veteran. The inexperienced player invariably will try for placements on the volley and more often than not fail to make them. The tournament-wise competitor will concentrate on placing her volley deep, thus trying for control of the situation.

One of tennis's most spectacular shots is the smash, but here again finesse may be more effective than power. Your opponent streaks for the back-court as you set yourself for the smash. She is certain the ball will be hit with terrific power, and if she gets back quickly enough she has a chance to make a return. Here, let's look at Vic Seixas, who is the greatest exponent of a fast change of pace. He hits a comparatively soft smash to the forehand court, with a lot of angle, thus completely throwing off his foe, who has gone deep expecting something else.

Perhaps in these pointers to the gallery, I have stressed my own strategy too much, making it appear as if I were a master tactician. That was my goal, although I did not always achieve it. It may have been that I played a 'gambler's game,' going for the lines, relying on power, speed and superb physical condition to carry me to triumph. Yet I tried for brains as well as brawn.

As you watch a match, there can be a subtle turning-point, and if you look closely it may often be detected. Since I first played, I looked for a 'sign.' To me, this was a mystical phenomenon, but you, of course, may observe it without recourse to 'black magic.' There may be a long rally, one player executes a seemingly impossible return, goes on to win the point. Then the fire can fade from her opponent's game. Watching closely for this, you may be able to predict the outcome of the match, long before it's over.

Physical condition can be the key to victory. There is no antidote for 'running out of gas.' I can cite a perfect example of this by giving you a brief description of the finals at the 1956 Pacific Southwest Tournament in Los Angeles. Nancy Chaffee Kiner, on the come-back trail, was pitted against Althea Gibson, who was winding up her biggest year on the courts. To the casual spectator, Nancy looked like a sure winner. In the first set, Nancy was master of the situation, but if one watched closely towards the end of the set, Nancy was breathing much harder than Althea, her condition was not as good and neither was her speed afoot. Yet Nancy had displayed the better strokes and won the set.

Then came the rout. Althea knew where her foe's weakness lay and exploited it, running Nancy from one side of the court to the other. Althea was certain that lack of condition would take its toll. It did. A keen observer could have forecast this accurately.

Now 'gamesmanship,' to crib a word. If anyone had a more natural inclination than I to flare up at bad calls, I never met her. I told you of my experience at Forest Hills, how I fashioned my own tennis philosophy. Still, the impulse to glare at an official and ask 'Myopia or astigmatism?' remained strong, but curbed. The girls, may I add, often in sharp contrast to the boys, maintain discreet silence.

I have made bad calls when I have served as a linesman. Yet my eyesight is perfect, my reflexes fast. To err is human, and tennis has no photograph-finish camera. This brings to mind an incident related to me by a turf official. He and his two associate placing judges had their eyes glued on a close finish. The three of them agreed a certain horse had been the winner. Yet when they looked at the photograph of the finish, this horse actually was fourth!

Girls are better sportsmen on the courts than boys, but they don't enjoy the game as much. Some of the howls at decisions by the boys are, I think, the result of sheer exuberance. Although Vic Seixas and Tony Trabert have been known to register bitter protests at decisions, neither approached Bill Tilden, nor do I know of a single boy or girl who used such behaviour as a weapon as Tilden did.

Sportsmanship meant absolutely nothing to Tilden, again using Les Stoefen as my source. Tilden had a dialogue unmatched in acidity and it had a single objective: to shatter his opponent's game. Whether the calls were good or bad, the ball boys dextrous or clumsy—all this was beside the point to Tilden. He enraged everyone, and most of all his opponent.

While I played big-time tennis, I never encountered studied psychological tactics. It is rare, indeed, even in a small tournament. Only once was I the intended victim of a mental attack, and this came in a small Western tournament in the United States. I was just beginning to twinkle faintly in the tennis firmament; my opponent had been a bright star, now fading. I can understand now, of course, the spectre of humiliation, the possible loss to an upstart in pigtails. She decided to stall, to delay the match at every turn, even to taking ten minutes out to repair a supposedly broken bra strap. I finally won in three long, close sets. Under ordinary conditions, I think I might have won rather easily in straight sets.

I have tried with might and main to behave impeccably on the tennis court, and I am sure that no matter what my inner emotions may have been they were never reflected by my outer conduct.

One more word about officiating, and a passing tip for the spectator. On grass, if a ball kicks up chalk, it is not necessarily good, although it's usually so called. The reason : a line may become smudged and a ball which really is out still can kick up chalk. (Officials, please note.)

'Water?' is the accepted one-word feminine dialogue on court. As you change courts and sip water you offer your opponent some, but nothing more. Preferable decorum for the girls is to double as a mummy. But with the boys, who enjoy the game more, it's different. I remember a French tournament when Budge Patty and Gardnar Mulloy had finished the first set and Patty told me he said jokingly : 'Boy, you were sure lucky in that last set. I'll wax you in this one.' For girls, this dialogue would be unthinkable, a reason for ostracism and truly a *cause célèbre*. Yet Patty and Mulloy, who are friends, thought nothing of it.

What should a girl wear on the courts? Dresses preferably! They're more feminine, look nicer and give one the feeling of being well groomed. Shorts and T-shirts are fine for practice, but in tournament play dresses are far more attractive.

From the time I was sixteen, Teddy Tinling, the world-famous London designer, made all my clothes, and anyone who has had to worry about the cost of a new dress can appreciate what a free wardrobe meant to me. He designed my tennis outfits, street clothes and ball gowns.

Teach Tennant introduced me to Teddy at the Longwood Cricket Club in Boston. Dress designers were catalogued in my mind as French, dapper and small. I wasn't prepared for Teddy. He towered over me, a robust, six-foot-plus giant, with greying hair and a moustache to match.

Primarily a designer of street wear and ball gowns for a fashionable London clientele, Teddy branched out into tennis dresses because he loved the game. He had been appointed a call boy at Wimbledon, which involved knocking on the dressing-room door and announcing the matches. One incident I remember caused an uproar. Teddy had designed an outfit for Kay Stammers Menzies, the English star, and now it was time for her match. She called through the door that she couldn't get her zipper to work. Teddy stamped impatiently outside. Time was running out. Unless Kay appeared, her match would be defaulted. This was an unhappy prospect, but to Teddy the imminent tragedy was she would not appear in his new tennis creation. Finally he could stand it no longer. He opened the door, strode inside, fixed the zipper in a twinkling, oblivious to the feminine shrieks and the dash for cover by a number of girls in various degrees of undress.

Gorgeous Gussie Moran, a beautiful American girl, was Teddy's undoing as a Wimbledon call boy. Teddy designed her celebrated lace panties, London officials took a few horrified looks and Teddy was relieved of his duties.

Teddy had two moments of small crisis with me. In the Wightman Cup matches at Wimbledon one year I walked on the court wearing a very tailored tennis dress with a satin collar and four satin tabs in front. I looked across at my opponent. She had on an exactly identical outfit! Teddy was so upset he wanted to postpone the match, but the fact he had designed the other girl's dress didn't bother me a bit.

I rebelled, however, at his idea of having me launch a new 'bloomer girl' fashion in tennis attire. I liked Teddy's dresses too much. He finally gave up on the idea and dubbed me his 'temperamental queen.'

My ideal tennis dress is sleeveless because it allows more freedom. Then I like a tight-fitting waist, which gives one a snug feeling. I prefer a wide skirt. It has more beauty with its graceful flare and it doesn't bind. Cotton and sharkskin, which absorb perspiration, are the best materials.

My favourite tennis dress?

It was really a creation, severely tailored, but the skirt set it off, as Teddy had designed a string of woolly poodles inset in organdie. Each poodle had a rhinestone eye.

I still wear it on special occasions.

CHAPTER SEVENTEEN

THIS IS MY TENNIS GALLERY. Let's tour together, look at a few portraits—legendary and contemporary—but keep in mind the fact we face a pitfall: comparison. This is inevitable, I suppose, but if I cannot bridge it then I should like to preface it.

Journalists must compare, it is part of their technique and, if their tenure is long on the tennis scene, 'I remember' is woven into their stories. There will come a day when a flashing little girl in pigtails will capture the tennis imagination, and the phrase 'Another Little Mo' will leap from the typewriter keyboards; stroke for stroke our games will be compared, dissected and editorially digested. There is no true yardstick to bridge space and time, bringing the champions of different eras into a sharp and clear perspective, but discussions will continue as long as there are tennis courts and players to bring them alive. It feels strange that I, at twenty-two, should be part of a tennis legend, a statistic in the record book long before my time. Well, let's look at our gallery.

Helen Wills!

There, for me, was sheer magic—the greatest of them all! It has been years since I first met her, but the memory remains bright and I can recapture the warm and happy feeling I experienced. No one reigned with the glory of Helen. I had pored over her remarkable feats in the record books. I had listened while Mom talked about her for hours. You see, my mother had played mood music for silent movies, and the newsreels were always full of Helen's triumphs.

I was twelve years old and playing in the fifteen-and-under age division in the Pacific Southwest Championships when my coach, Teach Tennant, told me she had asked Helen to watch me play and get her opinion of my game. I was mid-way through the first set when I glanced towards the sidelines and saw Helen and Teach standing together by a tall pillar watching me.

Instead of becoming nervous, my game caught fire. I played with flaming resolve, anxious to show Helen the best I had, eager to win her approval. I raced to victory in straight sets, could hardly wait to shake hands with my opponent before dashing over to Helen and Teach.

I had heard, of course, that Helen was reserved, a cool person. She had been dubbed 'Miss Poker Face.' I found her warm, gracious and charming without trace of aloofness. I still remember her lovely white dress, decorated with gold thread, and the large and attractive picture hat she wore. (Fortunately, I had a nice tennis dress, which Perry Jones had bought for me.)

'What do you think of Maureen's game?' Teach, always direct, shot the question almost before the introductions were over.

'Maureen will become the national champion in four years, and possibly the world's champion,' Helen answered. I was overwhelmed. Helen's prediction was calm, casual, almost as if she had looked into the future in some mysterious fashion and knew, with quiet certainty, exactly what lay ahead.

When I met her again, I was eighteen years old and had twice won the world's championship. We were in Perry Jones's office at the Los Angeles Tennis Club. Helen looked at me, smiled and asked: 'Do you remember?' (How could I possibly forget!)

'But,' I lamented, 'I still have no net game.'

'You don't need one,' she countered. 'You can beat any net-rusher. You are the first girl, I think, since my day who has decent ground strokes.' (Believe me, I was overawed. My titles meant nothing. For me, THE CHAMPION was speaking.)

'I believe,' Helen continued, 'I proved ground strokes could beat the best of the net-rushers, and you have proved it, too.'

Shortly afterwards, I played perhaps the strangest match in my career, because, for me, two time zones were involved—the past and the present—and they ran together. It was a mixed doubles match, and across the court from me was Helen Wills, a fact in itself incredible because she still was clothed in a legend. She had not been practising, her footwork was slow, she made errors. Yet she outguessed me at every turn!

It is difficult to describe a match such as this, because time ran backwards. I could visualize Helen's greatness, how she must have played at her peak, because now, many years after her tournament career had ended, there were flashes of her matchless form, fire in the embers of greatness.

Could I, at my best, have beaten Helen, at the top of her game? I do not believe I could. There are tennis writers who have said I could have beaten Wills, Lenglen or Marble, each at the pinnacle of her form. As I have said before, no true yardstick exists.

Judging strictly by the record book, Helen was in a class by herself. Perhaps I hit harder than she, moved faster, and my net game may have been a shade better. Against this were her tremendous cross-court angle shots, her flawless strategy, amazing steadiness and consistency. I, at my best, might have taken one or two matches from her, but to have beaten her consistently. . . . Well, I do not think the girl ever lived who could have done that.

Helen Wills, of course, is Mrs. Aidan Roark. Her husband, formerly a world-famous polo player, is now a prominent turf official. If tennis ever builds a shrine to Helen's memory, I should like to do my share of hero-worshipping.

Although Teach Tennant has developed a number of great players, Alice Marble was the first women's champion she sent to the tennis wars. Teach believed Alice was better than either Wills or Lenglen, and her highest compliment to me was: 'You'll soon be as great as Alice Marble was.' From the first day I went under Teach, I had Alice's prowess drummed into me, and I often think I could recite her record accurately from memory.

It wasn't, however, until I was fifteen that Alice saw me play.

It was at East Hampton, Long Island, in a match against Helen Perez, and I was having trouble. I managed to win in a long three-setter. Alice was not impressed by my game and she did not see a glowing future for me. Looking back now, I can understand her viewpoint.

Alice perhaps was the first really fine woman player with a man's game. She had the 'big serve' and followed it to net where her volley game was beautiful and deadly. I had neither Alice's devastating service nor anything resembling her volley. Teach, who was shaken by Alice's less than enthusiastic opinion of my game, did not tell me of this until much later.

However, Teach, as usual, decided upon direct action. A magic summertime wand would be waved and, presto, I would emerge as a flashing younger version of the incomparable Alice. Sweat, strain and tennis tears, however, were not enough. Teach was the instructor at the fashionable Bishop's School for Girls in La Jolla, California, and that summer the Italian Tennis Federation had sent her two Roman stars to polish. Alice was to assist in this undertaking, while my game would undergo revision.

Fausto Gardini and Giuseppe Merlo, now members of the Italian Davis Cup team, both presented problems to Teach and Alice. Neither player had anything resembling an orthodox game. Gardini had no form. Merlo choked his racket on a forehand and used a two-handed backhand. Teach tried, without success, to alter their styles, but both boys were too set in their strokes to change. Teach decided to improve the games they already had, which, of course, were good. We practised hard, played round-robins, and for me the emphasis was on the big serve and volley.

If Gardini and Merlo were frustrated (they disliked American food), I was doubly so, for a different reason. I had no big serve and I wasn't getting one. I would come to the net with a swooping rush after my serve and promptly would be passed by one of the Italian stars. In order for this type of play to succeed, the serve must blast the way for the volley shot. Mine didn't. I had no chance against either Italian player, yet if I stayed in the back-court and fought it out on my own terms I could hold my own against either of them.

It was a frustrating summer. After a practice session, I would often go to the Balboa Tennis Club and try out my new tactics. The results were sorry to behold. Boys whom ordinarily I might beat now trounced me easily. I should explain here that during a revision of strokes or tactics, one expects to lose. The concentration is upon improvement in a certain area and not upon winning. However, there is compensation. You know that when you master the new strokes or tactics your over-all game will improve. I, however, did not know this or believe it.

I appreciated what Teach and Alice were trying to do for me, and, had they been successful, I would have developed a more formidable attack faster than I did. But as my game kept getting worse, my belief increased that I wasn't ready for such a drastic change. Alice's serve was almost unique in women's tennis. She had more powerful shoulder action than I, she was taller and able to use her height to add power to her serve.

Psychology, too, was working against me. I had been hit in the chest by a hard smash at the net when I first started playing. That may have been a stumbling-block to my volley game. I had always been told 'how bad your serve is' and probably I came to believe it always would be bad. Shirley Fry, whose serve is her weakest weapon, had this same experience. For me, it wasn't until the eve of my retirement, when Les Stoefen was working on my serve, that I thought it might be good. Stoefen was convinced I would develop a tremendous serve; he believed it implicitly, and I was so impressed that I, too, believed. Another mental hazard to this new serve-and-volley attack was my inner conviction that both Helen Wills and Suzanne Lenglen had been superior to Alice and neither had built an attack on serve and volley alone.

Finally, as my game grew steadily worse, Teach and I had a long talk and I explained just how I felt. She decided we should abandon the new tactics and I went back to my old game, perfecting what I had, playing within my limitations. Later, I developed a volley game under Hopman, but it was based on coming in, not after a serve, but after a forcing shot where the return would be strictly defensive. This gave me the option of putting the volley away or running my opponent, whatever the situation dictated.

Teach believed that Alice had been the greatest women's champion, utterly invincible when she was 'on.' I would rank her below both Wills and Lenglen, although she might have beaten either at the zenith of her game. To me, a great champion does not score a brilliant win one afternoon, then lose to a mediocre opponent the next, as Alice often did. My champion must be consistently great, as Wills was. You could count her losses on the fingers of one hand.

Among today's great women players, Althea Gibson's game resembles Alice Marble's, and Alice, I understand, has helped Althea to some extent in her career. Althea has the big serve and deadly volley. Her ground strokes and back-court game have improved and are better than when I played against her. She's tall, and, like Alice, she brings her height into play as a power lever for her serve. When one plays Althea, it is a foregone conclusion her blistering serve will result in aces, but she will often serve double-faults, too. She is extremely graceful on the court, moves like a panther and glides rather than runs. Her legs are long enough to do this effectively and her footwork reminds me very much of the Swedish Davis Cup star, Sven Davidson.

Althea gained tremendously in international stature in 1956, her best year, and I'm sure her European tour has helped her game. I am not convinced she has yet acquired complete 'court savvy'—knowing exactly the right thing to do at the right time. She's a deadly opponent when she's ahead, but her game doesn't seem as good when she's behind, and I do not think she's the best 'clutch player' on the present scene. Her tennis was better in the opening rounds of Wimbledon than in the closing ones, but certainly the 'centre-court jitters' is an understandable thing. For Althea, 1957 could be the big year.

Shirley Fry, the 1956 Wimbledon winner, may be the most dangerous player today in women's tennis. She is perhaps the greatest retriever the game has ever known. She can return impossible shots and, as the case with Beverly Baker Fleitz, Shirley is more dangerous when she is behind. Her serve is weak, but oddly enough she has an amazingly good overhead and she can volley effectively if necessary. Her game is something like mine was—a reliance on power, good ground strokes and a fine back-court attack. Shirley has tremendous fighting spirit and is a fiery competitor until the last point is won.

Louise Brough, the California player, certainly ranks high on the list of champions. I beat her twice at Wimbledon, played her five or six times, losing only once, and that in the Southern California championships. I did not, however, meet Louise when she was at the peak of her career. When I flashed on the scene, Louise had started going down-hill, and I often felt she beat herself through nervousness. She's high-strung and there was the added pressure of knowing there had been a brighter, better day in her career. I have seen her become jittery when she served and sometimes it was necessary for her to throw up several balls before she hit one. I have also stood behind her and seen her racket waver because of nervousness. In her winning match against me, she got the jump, forced me and, I believe, gained quick confidence. She deserved to win.

Playing Louise, to a much lesser degree, was like having Helen Wills on the opposite side of the court. There would be flashes of great form and Louise might be tremendous for several games, but this was never sustained for an entire match.

Louise is a fine tactician, with an amazing variety of shots, great versatility and an uncanny change of pace. She has a good serve, excellent volley and a bold power game. She is the greatest doubles partner I ever had, the most magnificent 'poacher' that women's doubles has ever known. Poaching, as you perhaps know, is taking a shot intended for one's partner and the swift interception is usually made at the net for a quick point. Louise taught me the art of the lob and she was a past master at deception here, putting the ball over the opponents' heads when they were set for a hard shot down the middle. Ironically enough, I later used this tactic against Louise in singles. We played together in 1952 and although we beat Hart and Fry in some of the smaller tournaments, we lost to them in the big ones. Margaret Osborne du Pont, who was Louise's regular partner, was not playing that year. Louise, of course, would have been much more confident, and understandably so, with Margaret as a partner. Their team was the best, I think, in the history of women's doubles.

I played Margaret du Pont once during my career, and again it was a case of facing a player far from the pinnacle of her game. I beat her 6-1, 6-1, at Wimbledon in 1954, but the score does not tell the story. She was not in top condition, she had put on a bit of weight and was making a come-back after having had a baby. Yet, despite this, she was the most deceptive player I ever faced! I went for everything, but I could not anticipate her attack, although thanks to my youth and speed I was able to overpower it. Margaret has Louise's wide variety of strokes, yet she is a much calmer player and loses no points to nervousness.

After our match I said: 'Margaret, I have never played a match like this before. . . . I had no idea where the shots were coming.' She smiled, thanked me for the compliment and re-gretted she wasn't in better condition and hadn't been able to give me sterner competition. I, secretly, was thankful, because it was easy to picture her at the peak, and certainly her finest game would have been something no one would have relished combating.

Beverly Baker Fleitz, I thought, would win Wimbledon in both 1955 and 1956. She had beaten Louise Brough repeatedly in 1955, yet Louise rose to the heights at Wimbledon and van-quished Bev. Then, in 1956, Beverly withdrew when she learned she was pregnant. So it looks as if 1958 may be her big year.

Beverly is ambidextrous, and this unorthodox style of play has advantages and disadvantages. Her backhand is really a left-handed forehand, consequently it is a tremendous power shot. At first it is baffling to face this sort of attack. Beverly hits hard, puts her body into the shots, and from the back-court, she's one of the hardest hitters the game has known. She's quick, deft, and her racket-head travel is the fastest in tennis.

There are disadvantages to Bev's game. She burns up a tremendous amount of energy, and I've often thought she was more formidable at the beginning of a season that at the climax. She has trouble with balls close to her, and I think, although others don't agree, she is not effective with wide balls taken on the run. She has to change hands, she has a long backswing, and occasionally hits late. Her short game is nowhere near as dangerous as her back-court play, but recently she's tried a two-handed backhand volley shot. However, one should never under-rate Beverly—she's capable of beating any girl in tennis.

Of the English girls, I think Angela Buxton appears the best, and certainly her game has improved tremendously. She has youth in her favour, she's much younger than the top American girls, she has tremendous stamina and is a terrific fighter. Her game is well rounded, always dangerous. However, she does not appear to be a natural athlete, she moves rather stiffly and there is a need for more suppleness. I think she would improve under Hopman (who wouldn't!), and I believe ballet exercises would be a definite help. Here, may I say, to become a champion, it is not necessary to be a 'natural.' The classic example of this is furnished by boxing. Gene Tunney, who rose to be the world's heavyweight champion, was 'made.' He had a good body, little ability, but a flaming determination which carried him over all obstacles.

Lew Hoad, I think, is potentially the greatest tennis player who ever lived, and from the standpoint of athletics is the diametric opposite of Gene Tunney. Hoad is completely natural and relies upon his wonderful reflexes. Hopman and I have waged many an argument over Hoad. Hop thinks Lew is magnificent, a great champion, and much superior to Ken Rosewall. I disagree, and I differ because of Lew's lack of consistency. True, when he's 'on' he's unbeatable, yet he is often beaten by far inferior players—Freddy Huber of Austria, Michael Davies of England and Sven Davidson of Sweden, to mention three. Hoad is fantastically careless; his concentration is likely to waver at any time. But he has a beautiful build, is strong as a horse, and can use his big serve without tiring in the least. In 1956, he mastered a splendid return of service, using a short looping drive. He has powerful and supple wrists and he puts a lot of whip or pace into his shots. If he had a real knowledge of tactics, total concentration, . . . well, he would stand alone—perhaps for all time.

I think Rosewall is the better player, and this certainly is the minority opinion, but I have played with both boys. Ken has a touch of the classic game, plus the power of the modern game. He thinks well on the court, and some day he might beat Lew consistently; that day will come when Ken overcomes the psychological stumbling-block Hoad has posed. Lew knows exactly how Ken's serve bounces and he's set for it, and he has the mental advantage of a number of wins over Rosewall. But there may come a time . . .

Richard (Pancho) Gonzales, of course, stands out among the professionals, and, today, he is so good he's virtually put himself among the unemployed. Tony Trabert offered no competition for him. The only one today in the pro ranks who might give him competition is Frank Sedgman, the Aussie star who was the greatest amateur of my era. But Frank lacks colour, and only a tournament player could appreciate his effortless game. The gallery wants colour. Gonzales left me cold as an amateur, but his game as a pro shines and sparkles with brilliancy. He has the biggest serve in tennis; in fact, he has everything—he's a tremendous natural athlete. He is a fine example of what tennis can do for a youngster from the wrong side of the tracks, who without the inspiration of the game might have been a case number in a police file.

No tennis gallery would be complete without Bill Tilden and Suzanne Lenglen. Both, of course, were long before my time, although I did see Tilden play, years after his prime. For a brief portrait of Tilden, I rely upon Les Stoefen, the pro at La Jolla Beach and Tennis Club and formerly a world's champion doubles player. Oddly enough, Les's career began much like mine—he looked through a knot-hole in a fence and saw Tilden play in Hollywood at the height of Bill's career. This brief flash of inspired tennis impelled Stoefen to take up the game and he rose to the very top and even vanquished his idol, Tilden.

'Tilden,' Les told me, 'beat me in a pro tournament when he was fifty years old! He was in a class all of his own, there never was anyone quite like him, and when he quit mental warfare left with him. He would do anything to beat you—nothing was barred.

'Tilden,' Les continued, 'could break up the game of the finest player. He never beat himself. Bill was almost twenty years older than I when he beat me in this pro tournament. I had played him many times and I knew every trick in his bag. He began fuming at the ball boys, kicking at the calls, interrupting the match. I just laughed at him—it was all old stuff and didn't annoy me a bit.

'I had him down, 5-2, my serve, in the deciding set,' Les recalled, 'when he suddenly switched his tactics, started spinning and slicing everything. It threw me off completely. The gallery was spellbound. Then Bill, by some superhuman effort, lifted up his game and hit everything hard. There was never anyone quite like him.'

In France there is, and perhaps always will be, one great woman player—Suzanne Lenglen. This is by no means a strictly French viewpoint. Perhaps one of the reasons I was well received in Paris was because some French journalists wrote that my game was somewhat similar to Suzanne's.

Her court wizardry was not entirely a natural gift, because her mother and father decided she would become the world's best and laid out a strenuous training régime. Deadly accuracy was one of Lenglen's great weapons. Those who have played against her said she could hit a coin placed anywhere on the court. As a child, her parents marked off squares on the court and Suzanne practised for hours stroking the ball, hitting the targets.

Suzanne beat Helen Wills in a match on the French Riviera, but it was before Helen reached her peak. Perhaps no girl in the world was more colourful than Suzanne, to listen to the stories about her. She occasionally tossed off a split of champagne between sets, and then her father provided sugar cubes soaked in brandy for Suzanne to munch on for extra energy.

In the late 1920s, Suzanne turned professional and was guaranteed the then fabulous sum of $50,000 for one tour. She also had a percentage of the gate and the tour drew tremendous crowds. This enterprise was promoted by C. C. (Cash and Carry) Pyle, a flamboyant American sports promoter of that era.

My warmest French memory and the most sincere tribute to my game came from the French professional, Paul Feret, an old friend of Suzanne, who had made the first pro tour with her. Paul and I practised together, after he told me in gallant fashion: 'I would consider it an honour to play with you.' (The honour and pleasure, I assure you, were all mine.) The clay-court game has a set of problems all its own. My tendency was to over-hit and my footwork was not good. Feret taught me to glide on clay, to curb my over-hitting, but his greatest gift to my game was a short drop shot. He had worked with Lenglen on this; it was difficult and tricky, but it became a potent weapon for me.

Feret and I practised many times. Before I left France for the last time he told me: 'Maureen, your game more resembles Lenglen's than anyone I have ever seen. The others? No.'

It was my nicest French compliment.

CHAPTER EIGHTEEN

EVERY TENNIS PLAYER meets celebrities, just as a newspaper-girl does, and here I should like to introduce you to a few of my favourites. I have made friends in every part of the world I have visited. It seems to me that, if the day ever comes when no passports are required, no high trade barriers exist, that will be a day much closer to universal peace.

There is, I suppose, nothing quite like the pomp and solemnity of an audience with the Pope, yet my adventure might be a bit unusual in Vatican history. We were on tour in Rome, playing in the Italian championships, and everyone wanted to meet the Pope. So arrangements were made for about fifty of us to have an audience. The boys were to wear dark suits and the girls were to be attired in black or dark blue dresses. This came as a bomb-shell to Shirley Fry. The nearest thing she had was a beige sweater and skirt. (She wore them and the Pope didn't mind a bit!)

We had assembled in the huge Vatican square when an aide arrived with alarming news: the girls must wear either veils or lace shawls. So there was a mad rush to buy veils. Finally we were attired properly, escorted inside and as we walked down a long corridor I almost toppled over a priceless statue. The impressive setting was too much for me, but this near-accident was only a forerunner of what was to come.

We were divided into various language-speaking groups just before the audience, and we had to decide in what order the members of our group would meet the Pope. There was a quick and unanimous choice for the first person in line—Bernard (Tut) Bartson, an extremely devout Catholic. This surely was the greatest moment of his life.

The Pope appeared in resplendent white robes. He was much

smaller than I thought he would be, about five feet three or four, I should judge. He had the kindliest eyes I have ever seen and I can still remember him vividly. Our audience, at which we all received the Papal blessing, was in 1953, just a few days before the Pope's serious illness.

Bernard Bartson shifted from one foot to the other as the Pope approached, stopped, smiled and asked: 'And what country are you from?'

'I am from America, your Holiness.'

The reply was barely audible. I made it out because I was standing directly behind Bernard, whose voice froze. The Pope didn't catch it and said: 'Pardon me?'

Now Bernard's vocal cords suddenly loosened and he boomed 'Ah'm from Texas, suh!' Only iron-willed restraint kept everyone from going into hysterics, but the Pope took it with a good-natured smile.

I was next. His Holiness asked about my tennis and told me he was glad that I could come. As I made my responses, I began squirming. Mervyn Rose was directly behind me. He thought this a hilarious moment to pinch me. He did repeatedly until I took two short steps forward. In the background I could hear Nell Hopman's stage whisper: 'Shame on you, Mervyn!' The Pope remained unaware of my dilemma.

For me, theatrical people hold a special charm and their vivacity and love of life are contagious. Incidentally, many of America's movie stars are really fine tennis players. This may be due, as Eleanor Tennant believes, to the fact that actors are often quite emotional and have a bit of exhibitionism in their make-up. No tennis coach in the world has taught more film celebrities than Teach, and it was the late Carole Lombard who gave Miss Tennant her nickname. Carole kept saying, 'Yes, teacher, dear,' until the nickname stuck.

Teach thinks tennis is an emotional game, thus popular with film stars, who are often good at the 'serve and volley' type of play, which appeals to them because it is the most spectacular attack. They make excellent pupils because their careers so often depend upon 'taking direction' well.

I have a lovely cable-knit sweater made by Joan Crawford, which I inherited because it was too small for Teach. Joan is an excellent player with a fine forehand. Barbara Stanwyck is another good player and so is Gilbert Roland, my early Nemesis. His tennis resembles a strip-tease. He starts off with several pairs of trousers, a number of sweaters and a rubber girdle, and during a match he will shed most of his garments as well as a few pounds. Tennis is the reason he retains such a spectacular build.

Groucho Marx, of all Teach's pupils, was the most difficult, despite the fact that she was prepared for him and exercises dominance over her pupils. Groucho is a priceless wit off stage as well as on, and his steady stream of *ad lib.* remarks resembled a rehearsal more than a tennis lesson. He stopped Miss Tennant cold with this one : 'You know, Teach, I play tennis as well as any man twice my age.'

Once, Teach was giving instructions to a Miss MacDonald and she kept urging her pupil to show more speed, to go for her shots and she used a vocal 'needle' with telling effect. Finally, after Teach chided her for missing an easy shot, Miss MacDonald blew up with : 'Why don't you try hitting a high C?' The crack was temporarily meaningless until Teach's secretary explained that Jeanette MacDonald was the famous singer. Needless to add, Teach is not an avid moviegoer.

Some of the movie stars are even more beautiful off stage than on, and this is true of Grace Kelly, whom I met on the *Dial M for Murder* set. She is a charming woman, a trifle reserved, and her manner was in complete contrast to the bubbling Bob Cummings, who was working with her that morning. I am a rowing fan and Grace and I talked about her brother, Jack, a great oarsman. Grace told me that, despite her movie stardom, she thought she had been a disappointment to her family because she hadn't turned out to be a great athlete. She has unusual poise and dignity and I could picture her as being perfect in her new role as the wife of Prince Rainier.

Movie stars have 'fans' all over the world, but no fan, I am sure, worshipped Gordon MacRae more devoutly than I. I was not quite seventeen when I met him and I had just won the nationals. I was to play in the Pacific Southwest championships at the Los Angeles Tennis Club and I was staying at the Beverly Hills home of Gail and Corney Jackson. Gail is the former film star, Gail Patrick.

The Jacksons, both tennis enthusiasts, give an annual party for players and movie stars. This, to me, is the high-light of the tournament. Gail had asked me if there were anyone special I should like to have invited. Gordon MacRae! My reply was instantaneous; she smiled and agreed.

Here was my great opportunity to wear the slinky black dress I had bought at Forest Hills. I could visualize my entrance —a *femme fatale* floating down a spiral stairway, a sudden hush, then Gordon MacRae would see me! I raced upstairs, changed and modelled my black creation for Gail and waited for her critical approval. Well, Gail is not only beautiful and charming, but has a tremendous amount of tact and diplomacy. Slowly, gently and deftly, she manœuvred me into a fluffy white dress, which, of course, suited me. (Some day I am finally going to wear that black number!)

Came the party! I took an age fixing my hair and I dressed only for Gordon. I was late, but what an entrance! I came slowly down the stairs, then paused as I heard a voice say: 'Where's my Little Mo?' And there at the foot of the stairs was Gordon MacRae waiting to give me a friendly hug. (Gail directed that scene with the Ernst Lubitsch touch.)

I floated through the evening on a cloud. Gordon was my dinner partner and I was smitten at once. I chattered all the time and he went out of his way to be gay and amusing. During the evening he sang several songs. Then, as he was about to sing another, he stopped and announced: 'Now Maureen and I will sing a duet.'

We sang 'Somebody Loves Me' and it was a riot. Gordon, as you know, has a really wonderful voice, and I . . . well . . .

I invited Gordon to the tennis matches and he asked me to visit him on the set where they were making *About Face*. I accepted eagerly. My free day fell on September 17th and I arrived at the studio about ten o'clock and the morning was swelteringly hot. Gordon had been working under hot lights since seven-thirty and he was wearing a heavy woollen outfit. He must have been exhausted, but he insisted upon a tour with me. He showed me the various sets and then we came back and stopped in the centre of a huge sound stage. Suddenly Gordon stepped back and boomed: 'Okay, everyone!'

The entire cast and crew sang 'Happy Birthday' and no girl ever had a nicer present on her seventeenth birthday! Gail had told Gordon the anniversary was coming up and he arranged the rest. He came to see me play in the finals and sat in the Jacksons' box. I remember him looking down at me and smiling his encouragement.

As I've told you, my tennis hit peaks at Wimbledon and Forest Hills. There is always a let-down for the Pacific Southwest and I rarely have played my best tennis there. This time things were different. Gordon was my inspiration and I won.

I've met a great number of movie stars, and without exception they have been charming and real fun, but I am sure you can understand why Gordon MacRae is my all-time favourite.

One of the most unusual interviews I had when I was writing a column for the *San Diego Union* was with the American girl bullfighter, Patricia McCormick. She was a strange person, burning with an inner fire, determined to become a great matador. This, she believed, was her destiny, and it was a sad thing, best described, I think, by the comment of a Mexican bullfight critic, who said: 'What a pity this is, what great courage, but so little talent.' Patricia has been gored several times and her courage has far surpassed her ability even against small bulls. I am not a fan, or *aficionada*, as they are called, but I can understand the tremendous appeal bullfighting has in the Latin countries, where it is the great drama of death. As I remarked, there is a similarity between tennis strategy and the torero's tactics with the bull.

Now to London. Among my English souvenirs is an autographed photograph of the Duchess of Kent, who doesn't usually sign her pictures. My three encounters with the Duchess of Kent, all in the Wimbledon centre court, found me breathless, speechless and excited, while she remained completely poised and charming as she awarded the trophy. (And to think I almost ruined her coat!)

One extremely pleasant afternoon was spent at the Queen's Club, where I was the guest of Field-Marshal Montgomery. He is an avid tennis fan, great on tactics and strategy, and his remarks about the match in progress were unerringly accurate. I had seen so many pictures of him wearing his famous beret that I felt, as we had tea, as if I had known him for a long, long time.

On my first Wimbledon assignment for the London *Daily Mail* I had a strange encounter with a celebrity. I was sitting in the members' box, scribbling notes, trying not to miss a thing.

A distinguished-looking gentleman behind me remarked : 'My, you are working hard, aren't you?'

'I'm not a very good writer,' I told him. 'I have to race around to all the courts trying to get everything in my stories. But the really good tennis writers can turn out wonderful stories from the bar.'

(In this connection, some of the writers occasionally remain in the bar, send out a colleague to obtain notes, then rely on their background in tennis to write really sparkling stories. This has its counterpart in America where 'beat reporters' have a syndicate arrangement, alternating with the 'leg work.')

'You seem to work harder,' my new friend observed, 'at your stories than you did at tennis.'

I smiled. 'Tennis comes naturally, but writing doesn't.'

'By the way,' he said, 'I understand you and your husband have accepted our invitation for dinner tonight.'

'Oh, no,' I returned, somewhat alarmed. (We had a really important dinner engagement.) 'We are having dinner with Lord Rothermere, who owns the *Daily Mail*.'

He chuckled. 'My dear,' he replied in a kindly voice, 'I am Lord Rothermere.' (I was so embarrassed I could have gone straight through the floor. But we did have a really wonderful evening.)

Perhaps you have seen motion pictures of the 'Acapulco Death Dive.' It is a truly dramatic sight, a 'must' on the tourist's itinerary, and I didn't miss it on my Mexican tour. We took the short plane trip from Mexico City to Acapulco, and it was like going to a new and totally different country, from the high, thin air to the heavy, tropical and jungle-like setting of the famous seaside resort.

In the Latin countries, there is often a sheer and deep drop from the high lavish plateau of wealth to the canyon floor of bitter poverty. Acapulco, with its beautiful hotels, lovely and expensive homes, likewise has its share of hovels and filth, and here babies and dogs are everywhere. My introduction to the 'death dive' was roundabout, but as we drove through this poor section my companion pointed out one home which was constructed of unmatched packing boxes and looked as if it might collapse at any moment. 'That,' my friend said, 'was the home of Roberto.' I looked in some horror before asking who Roberto might be. He smiled. 'That will come later.'

The setting for the death dive is a narrow gorge, with steeply rising sides. The ocean waves roll in, hit and boil out again. This gorge is directly in front of the La Perla Hotel. The dive is a beautifully and carefully staged event. Suspense and drama build up as the diver, a tiny figure, goes up the side of the cliff. He carries a torch and as you watch him make his way upward slowly you are struck by the rugged setting and this man-against-Nature struggle. Eventually, he reaches a ledge near the top. Torches suddenly glow on the opposite side of the cliff. He puts out his torch. Then a spotlight picks him out, a lone, tiny, brave figure. There is a hushed moment of silence. Then he slices through the air, knifes into the water just after a wave comes in. You wait an eternity for his head to appear. I was fascinated. We had watched it from the dining-room windows of La Perla

*Maureen Connolly in 1952 in action against Thelma
Long, the Australian, whom she beat and then went
through to win the Lawn Tennis Championships at
Wimbledon for the first time*

While on their honeymoon, 'Little Mo' and her husband, Norman Brinker, arriving in England, where she covered the 1955 Wimbledon championships for the London 'Daily Mail'

which looked down on the scene. Later I was engrossed in conversation when a small, curly-haired youngster appeared at the side of our table.

'May I introduce Roberto?' my friend said.

Here was the diver who had reached the high goal of every little boy in Acapulco. Suddenly our table was surrounded by waiters; service stopped as the help paid homage to a hero. Roberto was small, wiry and eighteen years old. He had been diving—for money—for three years, although he had started to train for his profession almost as soon as he could walk. He was a member of a strange and highly exclusive trade union—the Acapulco Divers—whose membership is sharply restricted. Although some of the divers have been injured, he never had. As I watched him, saw his quiet, assured confidence, his friendly manner amid all this adulation, I admired him deeply, contrasting in my mind this luxurious setting with Roberto's first home. Life hadn't given him much of a start, but he's made the most of his single opportunity.

One of my great ambitions as a newspaper-girl was to meet General Eisenhower. I can't tell you how thrilled I was at the prospect of seeing him at the San Diego airport on his first visit there, when he was campaigning for the presidency. I was one of the reporters assigned to do a 'piece' on him. When the plane landed and taxied to a stop, there was a tremendous crush to reach the landing steps. I was somehow shoved almost into his face. I knew I must say something fast, get an 'exclusive' quote. I was so startled the only thing I could think of was : 'What did you have for breakfast?' I must have made this sound so important and breathless that he was momentarily off balance. Could there be a poison plot? Did I have secret information?

Then he realized he was talking to a cub reporter, overcome by the assignment.

'My dear,' he said, turning on that charming smile of his, 'I haven't had a chance yet to have breakfast.'

Some day I'd like to have a real talk with him.

6—FD

CHAPTER NINETEEN

HAVING BEEN ON BOTH SIDES of the typewriter, I hope I can offer a few tips to both readers and celebrities, and here I shall try to draw aside the inter-continental journalistic curtain a bit. However, if I were asked (which is improbable) to conduct a Press seminary for celebrities, I know of no sure rule which can prevent an occasional 'bad press.' I've had both kinds. It is disconcerting, by the way, to have friends pick up a newspaper or magazine and ask you, 'Is this true?' or, 'Really, I didn't know this before.' Then comes one's own long-winded effort to set the record straight.

Many sports writers, especially in the United States, are great authors at heart, with a true flair for fiction. They sometimes use mythical quotes, not having bothered to talk to the champion about whom they are writing. This can have a built-in bonus for the reader, making for interesting Press, because the writer is not handicapped by recounting banal remarks.

I was a trial to feature writers because I 'had been done' many times and there was no new angle that might make the story come alive. The writer, with me as his assignment, would stop first in the newspaper 'morgue,' or library, and read all the available clippings about my career. There wasn't much in the way of a 'fresh angle,' because I kept my thoughts and emotions rather tightly bottled. The writing trick, then, became to invent a new one, and quite a few stories, I presume, were contrived in desperation.

Thus I have had a full quota of semi-fictional pieces written about me, and, for the most part, I didn't object. Only when a story interfered with my personal life or contained something that might turn the gallery against me was there a quick denial. Here is a case in point : I was in Rome and a correspondent for one of the American wire services was assigned by his New York office to do a feature story on me. I never saw the gentleman. However, he did talk to Julie Sampson, who was on tour with me, and she told him : 'I can't speak for Maureen.'

That, however, didn't curb his imagination, or prevent a fictional interview. I was quoted as having said I was not interested in boys, any boy, particularly Norman Brinker, to whom I was engaged. Then I supposedly turned to Julie, smiled and remarked : 'Isn't it nice to be old maids at our age?' A cute quote, surely; likewise an interesting story, and the angle was dewy fresh.

Norman read the story in the United States, and to say he was upset is putting it rather mildly. He called me, and, after almost $100 in overseas toll charges, our romance was 'on again.'

Later there was another story, which was used widely, and even now I am asked about it. Here is the background : I had planned to turn pro and go under the banner of Jack Kramer. He believed Pauline Betz, who is married to the topnotch Washington, D.C., sports writer Bob Addie, would be a formidable foe for me on a pro tour. In fact, Kramer thought Pauline might beat me. She had come out of retirement to vanquish Doris Hart in three sets, after Doris had turned professional. So a 'story' came out and was picked up by the wire services that Pauline and I had played a practice match and she had beaten me. The purpose of the piece, of course, was to stir up interest in a pro tour, but I, at the time, did not understand the workings of advance publicity. I was furious. I never had played against Pauline in a match; in fact, never so much as rallied with her.

There is a school of American thought about publicity, which includes the phrase, 'just so they mention my name,' and 'every knock is a boast.' The great fear here is 'the thunder of silence,' because the Press can create heroes, building them out of ink and type until they assume fantastic proportions. This fact naturally has a quick cash value at any box office for the athlete who might wish to turn professional.

My advice to the reader, when in doubt: Set your eyeglasses at a cynical slant. My word to the celebrity is: Be honest with the Press. It may seem clever at the moment to give out two different 'exclusives' to a pair of rival journalists, but the backlash from their typewriters can be stinging. For readers of the doings of the American motion picture stars: Prepare for entertainment only.

Tennis poses definite Press problems. I went through two phases—on the way to the top, and then at the top. The pressure, of course, is much less on the rising player than on the champion. It can be disconcerting, by the way, to explain a match to a sports writer who is supposed to know his subject. This has happened to me, but only in the United States, and only in some of the smaller tournaments. However, such explanations can pay dividends for the player.

The fact that I had a clear understanding of the responsibilities of journalists and photographers to their newspapers did not mean I could solve the problem of perfect relations. A reporter wants his story, a photographer wants his picture, but more than anything else I wanted to win, to remain the champion. This can cause a conflict of interest, often strained relations.

Concentration, the total kind I strived for, is not something that can be turned on and off like a water-tap. Before a big match, I wanted to think only of the struggle ahead, and an interview could prove a disturbing distraction. Then, right after a match, I did not want to give out an interview, for two reasons. My body was my bread and butter and I took care of it. The heartbeat speeds up during a match, and after one was over I wanted to keep moving, even in the dressing-room, until my pulse hit a normal beat and my breathing became regular. It is taxing on the heart, I think, to come to a dead stop, and, of course, there is the chance that muscles will stiffen (even fibrositis might set in, heaven forbid!) if you sit down after a match for a Press conference.

The other reason was that I would become keyed sky-high emotionally, and if I said anything right after a match it might easily have been the wrong thing. I might have been seething inwardly because my forehand had not been working right. Suppose I had been beaten, my inclination would have been to blame my forehand, yet, a later, cooler and more accurate analysis of defeat would have been that my opponent had exploited my weakness and had deserved to win. A quote in the heat of battle could and has put many a player in a bad light.

Photographers? First, bear in mind that they are dear to their mothers, wives and children. Then exercise patience. Truly, they are not fiends. If you are a tennis player, it is the better part of long-range wisdom not to go for a wide placement if it means bowling over a charming photographer in the process. Then, just when you are concentrating on the match at hand, 'Big smile, please,' can be a bit disconcerting, but still it may make a fine picture.

Most of my trouble with photographers came in the smaller United States tournaments, but there has been a spot of bad feeling, too, in the bigger ones. The rally, to me, is a deadly serious thing, a chance to probe for the weakness an opponent may have on a given day. The rally, for some photographers, is a moment to move in close, and this can be distracting.

Then, again, in a big match, the sharp click of a close shutter can have the effect of throwing off split-second timing; and my timing had to be perfect because when I was on top of my game my shots were hitting close to the lines. I wanted to feel as if the court were somehow isolated in space and my opponent and I were the only people in the world at this given moment in time. That's an idea of the concentration I sought.

'Prima donna' was a temporary tag I received because of a photographer, although it might stretch one's imagination a bit to picture an eighteen-year-old prima donna. However, the New York papers gave this a journalistic ride. 'Did she have a swelled head?' Or, 'No, she didn't,' and, 'Yes, she did.' The reader could buy his paper and take his choice. (The material about me must have been thin, indeed.) The stories grew out of an incident which occurred when I was playing in the Wightman Cup matches at the Westchester Country Club in Rye, New York. I arrived late on the courts. A photographer wanted some shots and I posed for a few stills. Doris Hart, Louise Brough and Shirley Fry were waiting for me, as we had arranged a practice session. Now the photographer wanted special action shots. I explained I was late and would be happy to have them taken later. He returned to his paper, a bit irate no doubt, and I became a 'prima donna' immediately.

Now, let's examine the 'bad Press.' I had two unfortunate experiences in Australia. First, I was charged with professionalism. Next, I was accused of refusing to practise with the Australian girls, and in this criticism Harry Hopman received some of the blame. Professionalism? I was covering the Davis Cup matches for the *Melbourne Herald*, and, of course, I was paid for the stories I wrote. However, this is permissible if one is not playing in the tournament about which you are waxing oracular on the typewriter keyboard. Naturally, I was not playing in the Davis Cup matches.

The other charge was partly true. As I told you, the prime reason for my coming to Australia had been to go under Hop's coaching. The Aussie boys offered far more competition than the girls. However, I did play with the girls, but their idea of a hard work-out consisted of a few short minutes of tennis, then a number of long minutes over tea. They simply did not take the same head-on approach to tennis I did.

London in 1952 provided my all-time 'bad press' climax, and looking back now I don't see how I could have avoided it. I was only seventeen, hardly a veteran at Press relations, and my mother, who was with me, had little or no experience with metropolitan journalism. Teach Tennant, my coach, on the other hand, was a seasoned pro with the Press, extremely articulate, and her story carried much more weight and got across far more clearly than mine.

However, may I say the English tennis writers are the best in the world; the London tournament coverage is unsurpassed, and for the player and keen follower of the game there is nothing like reading a deeply perceptive story about a match.

But page one in London! That can be an ordeal. There is more than a touch of sensationalism in some of the papers. Competition is keen on a fast-breaking story. I had broken with Tennant, I had fibrositis, and, although some of my tennis didn't indicate it, I was the American champion. My troubles became a daily diet and the reader must have been sated. I was. If there were no news, it was manufactured. I felt like a medical curiosity as doctors, osteopaths and chiropractors were quoted at length.

However, the friendships I have formed with journalists all over the world remain warm and pleasant memories, and a big scrapbook can be a glowing thing.

My favourite sports writer is Nelson Fisher. He is one of my dearest friends, and his wife, Sophie, as I told you, has travelled with me on tour and was always kind, understanding and sympathetic. Nelson has been my friend since I first started to play, he has given me sound advice throughout my career, often acting as a Press buffer, arranging interviews, TV and radio appearances. He is an extremely unusual and gifted sports writer as he is not only an expert on horse racing, boxing and tennis, but he is the only turf writer I know who 'beats the races.' Nelson is big, friendly, extremely generous, and although racing has been his exclusive assignment in recent years I would rank him with Allison Danzig of New York as a tennis expert. You have no idea what it means to have a friend who knows 'the tennis ropes' and whose prime interest in the game was my career.

Nelson and I both share the distinction of being 'Kentucky Colonels,' an honorary title, which has been widely conferred. Nelson always covers the Kentucky Derby—America's most famous horse race—while I became a Colonel following a Louisville exhibition. I still have a 'gag' photograph showing me decked out in a tall silk topper, a cane in one hand and a tall, frosty mint julep—Kentucky's favourite drink—in the other.

I met Nelson first when I played in the Ink Tournament in San Diego and he was assigned to cover the matches. He picked me out unhesitatingly, before I had won, sought background material, and his was the first 'expert' story about me—the forerunner of hundreds more.

It was Nelson who dubbed me 'Little Mo' when I was twelve years old. The American battleship *Missouri*, you may remember, became stuck in the mud—a famous nautical incident—and this gave Nelson the idea. He wrote a clever feature story, comparing my strokes to the armament and fire-power of the 'Big Mo.' The name stuck.

Nelson knew that newspaper copy-desk men, the ones who write the heads over stories, are partial to short names. He was looking far into the future when he believed I might be making international sports headlines and he was preparing the way. 'Little Mo,' or just 'Mo,' became an instant hit with headline writers, and I may have been their favourite tennis player, just as Ike became their favourite president.

Nelson was with me during most of the big moments of my career, and only he predicted in print that I would become the youngest American champion in history, and on that glorious day at Forest Hills when I won the title at sixteen, Nelson covered the story. Again, at Wimbledon, just before I took the court against Thelma Long in the semi-finals, a moment of ebb tide, Nelson arrived.

Nelson made friends with some of the English writers and he was quoted 'tipping' me in the London Press. My Press began getting better after Nelson's arrival. The journalists were struck by Nelson's honest and forthright manner, and, of course, he was an 'authority' and could answer any question swiftly, accurately and intelligently. The coverage, by the way, on my second and third Wimbledon wins was truly wonderful.

It was Nelson who launched me on my newspaper career, and the start of it caused him a spot of embarrassment. I've always admired newspapermen and was fascinated with the profession. I asked Nelson if he thought he could get me a job on his paper—the *San Diego Union*—and he told me there perhaps might be a good chance. So, after winning the United States nationals at Forest Hills, I was asked by the Press what I planned to do next. 'I'm going to work for the *San Diego Union*!' I announced proudly.

This was carried by the wire services. Nelson read it with some misgivings, as he had neglected to inform the *Union*'s editor of this great journalistic windfall. Nelson, however, got busy in a hurry.

Arriving in San Diego, I went to see the editor, Richard Pourade. 'I understand,' he remarked with quiet humour, 'you are going to work for us?'

'I hope so,' I returned tremulously.

'Well, I'd better find a job for you,' he said, and my fears dissolved.

I became a 'copy boy'—probably the world's worst. I managed to mislay stories, be late with coffee for the staff, contributing to the general confusion, but I truly loved the atmosphere of the city room. The staff kidded me constantly, and my first 'story' contained my impressions of my fellow workers and I paid them back in print in a humorous piece. This paved the way for 'Letters from Little Mo,' a feature that Mr. Pourade suggested I write on tour. Later, I did a sports column from the women's angle and an occasional magazine piece.

My most thrilling newspaper assignment was covering Wimbledon for the London *Daily Mail*! Here I felt I had really reached the top, working for one of the world's great newspapers, enjoying every minute of it, although my 'deathless prose' came hard. I discovered at once I was too critical a tennis writer and I had a sudden loss of popularity among some of the top women players. I watched the matches with a critical eye and I not only wrote what I saw but I worked in what I knew about the players. I had met most of them before and I knew what their games should be, and now, without the pressure of playing, I could see much more and with a clearer eye. I tried only for constructive criticism, nothing sensational, nothing derogatory. This did not win tennis friends, but instead created a bit of ill feeling. Not all the girls had the same reaction to criticism I did. As a player, I had been anxious for Hop to dissect my game, analyse the mistakes, and I profited by it, just as I gained by reading stories by top tennis writers who had pointed out flaws in my play. I was no stranger to the centre court, and any criticism I made of a player was in the spirit of lending a hand to her game. I found out it was a bit difficult to keep one's editor happy and stay friends with all the players at the same time.

Wimbledon TV was fun, as in addition to my *Daily Mail* assignment I also became a television commentator. My previous television and radio experience had been a reverse role, but now I was asking the questions instead of answering them. I loved it. Before the matches started, I had a five-minute spot in which I discussed the previous day's play and what I thought might happen in the matches coming up. I had luck in the oracle league as I was the only one in 1956 who predicted Shirley Fry would win. 'I think Shirley has all her fight and determination back . . . you know, I think she'll win,' I told Norman, my husband. 'Don't,' he advised, 'stick your neck out so soon.' I did, however, and in this prediction I was greatly assisted by the stork who took Beverly Baker Fleitz out of the tournament.

Then, when the matches were on, I had two twenty-minute spots in which I described the court action. There was, at times, a bit of electronic confusion. We had two cameras, switching from one to the other as they covered the centre and No. 1 courts. I sat in a small booth where there was a TV monitor set on the floor; I was supposed to watch this and comment solely on the action shown on my screen. However, I would get excited, look out on the courts, see a beautiful bit of play and remark: 'What a wonderful shot!' I did this several times, but I was not describing the action the camera was recording! I had earphones and I received instructions, a few of them frantic, from the director. Then, at times, I would indulge in an impromptu talk with the director, forgetting the conversation was going over the air. This made for many moments of hilarity, quite spontaneous, but the audience, it seems, enjoyed the novelty.

I love working on TV and have never had 'mike fright,' although I have a tendency towards rapid delivery, and 'Slow down!' would be an occasional directorial command over the earphones.

Recently I took a course in public speaking, but when I become excited my words volley like balls off a racket. I fear I shall never become a calm tennis commentator or a detached tennis writer. Too much internal combustion, I suppose.

CHAPTER TWENTY

THIS IS NOT INTENDED to be a 'kiss and tell' episode about professional tennis players masquerading in amateur garb, but, I hope, a sincere plea for understanding and sympathy for the exploited athlete. It's a delicate subject, taboo in some tennis circles, but I write with no eye cocked on possible headlines, and with no desire to 'name names' or furnish sensational testimony. I would like to keep this in a subdued and thoughtful vein.

It should, of course, come as no shock to you to learn that amateur is virtually a word with little meaning in the lexicon of big-time American athletics. An amateur, once upon a time, meant someone who played only for the love of sport. Today, the true amateur ranks in obsolescence with the dodo. If you see the name of a star athlete in United States headlines, you may be sure he's a pro and the question is only one of degree. These cold facts of hypocrisy are known, too, by those in charge of whatever amateur sport may be involved.

On the altar of American amateur sanctity, the scapegoats burn at intervals. These sacrificial offerings are usually accompanied by scare headlines, righteous quotes from regents, boards of governors, etc. It's a pat performance; the lines, trite and tearful, are never muffed. They've been repeated too many times.

The promotion of amateur American athletics is business, big business, and the sterling hall-mark of success is the high 'take' at the box office. Stadia are not built or filled by happy amateurs ready to do or die on the greensward for old Alma Mater. I have been closely associated with amateur athletics, written about them and have known many players in the sports-page drama. Before we delve into play-for-pay tennis, let's look over the field a bit.

The contract of an American college football coach has only the life expectancy of his winning streak; the number of times he can put his team into a post-season 'bowl' game, and these colossal spectacles are part and parcel of football. Pressure is intense. The coach not only has to be a skilled field-marshal, but he is also expected to play a leading part in recruiting his own troops. He wants a winning team, naturally, and the ethics of the so-called amateur code play little part in how he obtains his players.

Pressure, too, is heavy on the player. He must deliver on schedule. How can one possibly argue that it is legitimate to pay a player $75 a month, but illegal to pay $150? As I write this, the American colleges, the ones who field 'big time' football teams, are in the process of soul-searching. The Pacific Coast Conference had an upheaval; schools were fined for infractions; players were slapped on the wrist and the number of games they could compete in during the 1956 season was curtailed. If hypocrisy had an odour, it would engulf Californian football.

A much more comprehensive analysis of the situation was made by the 'Big Ten' Conference, which embraces the leading colleges of the Mid-West. Here a plea was made to recognize the situation as it exists, establish a legitimate schedule of free scholarships, supply bona fide employment to players, based upon individual need. Certainly, if America's football schools adopted a reasonable code, had an honest interchange of information, then the hypocrisy could be cut to a marked degree.

The star football player, of course, has a financial future as a professional, but what about the track and field champion? He is under a killing training routine; he may injure his heart from over-training, and, aside from a look at his trophies, he has no future as a professional. Yet, as an amateur, he's often exploited to the hilt.

The case of Wes Santee, an American track star, looms monumental in the hypocrisy division, and this is by no means the minority viewpoint of one girl. It was graphically high-lighted in the remarks of a trial judge. Wes was barred for life as an amateur, and yet had he not bickered with the American Amateur Athletic Union one wonders if such stern action would have been taken.

I was at a sports dinner given by the *Los Angeles Times,* and this supposedly was the setting for a run-in Santee had with a member of the A.A.U. To any seasoned athlete, the cause for argument was ridiculous. Wes objected to the timing arranged for the United States team's trip to Mexico City, where the Pan-American games would be held. It was decided to send the team to Mexico City a week before the games. This, naturally, wouldn't permit the athletes to become properly accustomed to the high altitude or the abrupt change in food and water. The Mexican 'turista bug,' which brings on a stomach upset, usually hits the visitor in the first two or three days. Wes wanted the team to go down a month before the games, which was the logical and safe course. Well, the argument grew bitter; Wes lost it. But more to the point, this, I am sure, was a strong underlying reason for the subsequently violent official attack against him. I know and like Wes. I am sure he has the sympathy of every American athlete.

Now, let's take a searching look at tennis.

To play tournament tennis, one must train and travel. Four hours of intensive daily practice constitutes much more work than eight hours behind a desk, and the player who fails to practise regularly never reaches the top. Is there any financial allowance made for practice? None. However, if a player has family responsibilities, his bills continue mounting.

Legitimate amateur expenses include from $15 to $20 a day living costs, plus transportation allowance. Yet a first-class hotel room in most of the world's capitals costs $12 a day. Athletes need red meat, and a steak dinner often runs to $6. If a tennis player is expected to be a credit to his country, he should be well dressed, and, of course, there always are travelling incidentals.

Unless a tournament player comes from a wealthy family, he faces a financial stone wall, and not many tennis champions are from the homes of the rich.

By necessity the tennis player becomes a sharp businessman. Some players ask and receive money for an 'appearance.' This may run from $400 on up to $1,000—depending upon the player's pull at the box office. None of this, of course, is red hot and breathtaking news in tennis circles, yet in the ostrich-like inner sanctums of tennis it is not mentioned.

Ironically enough, official punishment for tennis violations is often imposed by men who have been a party to 'under the table' payments for appearances. In the matter of suspensions, it might be an eye-opener to note that they are often lifted on the eve of an important tournament.

'How much can we get?'

This was the operative business motto of two amateur champions I knew, who, by the way, have not played tournament tennis for a number of years. For them, each tournament demanded new business strategy—an advance play calculated to bring the high dollar. Their long-distance phone calls (collect) to tournament officials were designed for sympathy and cash— Mother needed immediate hospital attention; their car had broken down and they were stranded—and so it went on, this complex scheme to get more appearance money.

I believe in all sincerity that I was the closest thing to a Simon-pure player in modern tennis history. Perry T. Jones, as I told you, arranged and approved my tournament itinerary, and not only is Jones scrupulously honest, but he believes in absolutely accurate accounting. The financial details of my trips and tours were set down like a bank statement and they balanced to the penny.

Fortunately, I was able to augment my expenses by newspaper work, and believe me I earned what I made. I worked hard over the typewriter. Writing what I thought might be an acceptable story was often more difficult than a hard match. However, I was censured in Australia, as I mentioned, for taking typewriter in hand.

My wardrobe problems were solved by Teddy Tinling, and if it hadn't been for Teddy I wouldn't have had a decent stitch.

This also drew official criticism. Teddy held a Press conference and an annual style show a week before Wimbledon and I modelled tennis dresses for him. The third year I did this, I received a cable from the United States Lawn Tennis Association, which in effect said : 'Naughty, naughty!' Yet there was no covering letter saying the U.S.L.T.A. would furnish me with a gown to wear at the Wimbledon Ball.

Twice during my championship career I asked for and received 'appearance money' above and beyond legitimate expenses, and each time I acted alone. I make no excuse here for such conduct. The fact that it was 'being done' and in current fashion certainly does not make it right, nor does the fact that the family bank account was at a low ebb alter the moral involved. I received $400 for a tournament in a Latin country and a similar amount for another in the United States.

I had decided definitely to turn professional before the accident which ended my tournament career. I wish neither to express nor to imply censure for amateurs who, to some degree, play for pay. In my case, I simply wanted to make it above board and considerably more than the going amateur rate.

The life of a tennis-playing professional is sharply limited, and this area of employment is definitely restricted. A brief burst of glory as an amateur champion does not necessarily mean a sunburst of success on the pro circuit. Dozens of great amateurs have failed to make the grade on pro tours.

Now we come to classic irony in double measure. 'Pancho' Gonzales, the world's ranking pro and the best tennis player in the world today, is losing his value as a draw at the American box office because virtually every tennis fan has seen him play. He received perhaps $15,000 in 1956. Jack Kramer, under whose banner Pancho plays, wanted new blood. He tried to sign Lew Hoad for a reported $100,000, but Hoad turned down the offer. Ken Rosewall likewise refused a handsome bid. Both thought they could do better as amateurs! Thus the 1957 Kramer tour is in a spot of peril. Tony Trabert, the American champion who turned pro, was over-matched against Gonzales, and while one might admire Tony's fight against a more formidable adversary, he was not much of an asset at the box office. Then, there's Rex Hartwig, who was almost excess tennis baggage on the tour. Yet, as an amateur in Australia, he still would be great.

For a still more striking example, take Frank Sedgman. He was a national idol in Australia. The tennis fans couldn't do enough for him, buying him an expensive petrol station, giving him a $12,000 wedding gift. He was the world's champion. He had a fine position with a sporting goods firm, his financial success as an amateur definitely assured.

And so he turned pro. Sedgman toured with Kramer's troupe. A great player, he lacked a single pigment of colour which might capture the fancy of the gallery. A tennis star who knows the game would pay gladly to see Sedgman's effortless play, but the crowd demands a flashier game and thus Sedgman was a bust. His popularity in Australia, of course, nose-dived, and today as a pro he's virtually a nonentity.

Well, let's look at the Australian amateur tennis system, which, I think, is head and shoulders above the United States system. A star may work for a sporting goods firm and receive good pay, although the work is largely a matter of reflected prestige to the firm coming from the player's court successes. Thus, in effect, an amateur is paid and paid well; he has no financial worries and he occupies a position of respect and admiration in his country.

Pro tennis is virtually non-existent in Australia. The prestige is for the amateur, and when he finishes a long and strenuous career he is not cast aside but held in national esteem. He experiences no difficulty in finding a good job or holding the one he may have.

American tennis faces serious threats on all fronts—particularly from Australia and Russia. The Aussie threat, of course, is a clear, present danger and constitutes more than anything else a kingly reign over Davis Cup competition. But what of Russia? As I write, they haven't been accepted yet into the Davis Cup field, but the Bear is advancing, racket in hand, and if Olympic competition is a criterion it will be a savage assault.

'Produce tennis champions!' It may be facetious to suggest such an order might emanate from the Kremlin, but a command in even a minor key would harness an awesome amount of man-power. And there will be no worry about the rouble for the tennis stars involved. The Soviet athlete or artist occupies a special position, and again there is national esteem and with it special privilege.

America is a nation where no premium is placed on being second best. Well, the governing fathers of all the tennis asso-ciations in the world are aware of the facts of tournament play. I say with all sincerity: drop the mask of hypocrisy. Pay the players a standard fee. Allow them to have jobs where their tennis prowess helps the firms for which they work. Do this above board. Adopt an international code which has meaning, and 'appearance money' would vanish overnight. The 'tennis bum,' a pathetic figure on the American scene, would dis-appear. The steady decline in United States tennis would end; there would be a mad rush of new hopefuls to the court, eager to reach the top, certain no financial worry would hinder their climb.

Or continue the *status quo*, and you will have this situation:

A youngster, imbued with every fine attribute of athletic competition—fair play, honesty, good sportsmanship—starts rising in the tennis firmament. As his star soars, as he begins playing in the major tournaments, his eyes come slowly open and he sees the sordid financial facts of tennis life. He becomes cynical or mercenary, perhaps both, and the true purpose of amateurism has been crushed and defeated. What has been gained? Who has been fooled?

My plan may sound commercial, but I know it will find favour with tennis stars; I know it will be endorsed by any really good tennis writer in the world. I know, too, it would make the land of big-time tennis a happier, healthier place with a better moral climate.

CHAPTER TWENTY-ONE

LET'S TAKE THE COURT for a 'how to do' session without pain, strain or diagrams. This exposure won't make you a great player, but neither will it hurt your game. Championship tennis and social tennis are worlds apart. Each is played with racket and balls, but there the similarity ends. So, in this chapter, you may choose your own brand of court warfare.

Tournament tennis means living, breathing, eating the game, thinking of nothing else, lying awake figuring how you may improve, how to correct your mistakes. Out of roughly five hundred tennis players, one is destined for the tournaments. He is the *rara avis* of the courts, obsessed with the game, propelled towards the top by a driving inner compulsion. Sometimes he makes it, but more often not.

Because of this, my début as a tennis instructor at San Diego's Town and Country Club was disastrous. I charged forth determined to transform a young businessman into another Lew Hoad or fashion a society girl into my *alter ego*. This may be like getting a saddle horse ready for the Epsom Derby. I lost pupils with amazing regularity, and I was baffled, but not my husband. 'Look, darling,' Norman said gently one evening, 'these people want a pleasant outing, a little exercise . . . they don't want to become tennis champions.' Then he added a bit sternly : 'Take it easy. Don't run them ragged.'

Norman, of course, was right, but it simply had not occurred to me that anyone, with racket in hand, did not want to become the best player in the world. The doctrine of perfection may be a fine thing, but the teacher should use it sparingly. So I changed my professional stance and my pupils wore happier expressions. Still, frustration gripped me at times. It's difficult for me to see a casual player, endowed with a perfect body, grace, co-ordination and good strokes fail to show more than a passing interest in the game. Here, I keep thinking, is a potential champion, but, alas, the spark is lacking.

My most shattering disappointment came at the start of my teaching career, when Barbara Breit, an eighteen-year-old Los Angeles girl, wanted to come under my wing. I was overjoyed. Barbara regarded me as her tennis idol just as I had placed other girls on a high pedestal. I worked hard with her and seemingly she had everything—fine strokes, power, court craft and a strong body. She had defeated Louise Brough in straight sets, and the world of tennis was her oyster, so I thought. But for Barbara the essential day-in and day-out drive was lacking; a big tournament career became secondary to her personal life. She was beaten in the 1956 Pacific Southwest Tournament, going down in sharp and crushing defeat. She became discouraged, fed up with tennis, and put her tournament rackets in moth-balls. I helped Barbara with her game, but much as I liked her I could not furnish the fuel and fire to power a flaming will to win.

I have two methods of teaching. One is for the prospective tournament player, the other designed for purely social tennis. If Wimbledon is the far goal, then the foundation must be perfect, and this often means a total revision of strokes, because there cannot be the slightest error in a ground stroke. If the pupil is serious, only work, hard work, lies ahead. The road to Wimbledon is paved with thousands of hours of practice. Even the seemingly perfect game is not enough. Too many players have fine games and flawless shots. For the champion, condition is essential, the kind of condition Harry Hopman demands of the Australian team, and that means road work, exercise as well as practice. But all this, the perfect game, the zenith of condition, cannot make a great champion unless there is the flashing competitive spirit, the overpowering desire to be the best.

Teaching social tennis can be a trial to the spirit. I might correct a mistake with painstaking care and tell my pupil to practise before the next lesson. Then, at the following session, the original mistake shows up again; there had been no inter-vening practice. I keep reminding myself: It's all in fun, don't become too serious. With the casual player, it's best to take the strokes he has, polish and improve them. His game becomes better; he enjoys it more, and there is no ordeal of total revision.

When should your child learn to play tennis? This question is asked often, and my preference is between ten and twelve. By then children's bones are formed, their bodies strong, and their minds alert enough to concentrate on what is being taught. There are exceptions, and at the moment I have an unusually strong and apt seven-year-old pupil. With children, a light racket is essential. At any age, poor instruction, or none at all, is a serious handicap, because then the game is built on such a faulty foundation that it may take years to correct the mistakes.

In America, the average free school instruction is exception-ally poor. A school athletic coach may supervise half a dozen different sports, and tennis is often the one he understands least. This criticism is not intended to point a finger of blame at the coach. By and large, he does a marvellous job of interesting youngsters in athletics, and if he does not know the fine points of tennis he may be excused. He is probably an expert on football, baseball and basket-ball.

I've had many graphic examples of coaches explaining their systems of teaching tennis. I'd stand and shudder at the ground-work of errors they were laying. In this connection, it is my hope that the Wilson Sporting Goods Co., for whom I work, will arrange for me to give tennis clinics for coaches. Now, my clinics are devoted exclusively to juniors, but by including coaches the field would become much wider and far more effective.

As a prelude to our court session, I'd like to refer you back to the 'clock' system which I discussed earlier. I use this in my teaching; it's effective and once learned it becomes a trusted stand-by, a point of reference, which always sweetens a sour shot. Well, take your racket. Shake hands with it like an old friend, firmly, but don't crush your friend's knuckles. If you find your grip isn't strong enough, we'll exercise at once. Squeeze a rubber ball just as a boxer does. If your wrist is weak, use a light bar-bell weight.

For the forehand, we'll use the eastern grip, and that's just shaking hands with your racket. Your 'drop' backswing will go straight back; when you become a more advanced player, you may use a loop backswing. Stay on your toes or, more accurately, the balls of your feet and be in perfect position. Now, remember this! Watch the ball with a concentration so complete you can see the seams. Hit an absolutely flat shot, with the backswing and follow-through based upon the 'clock' system. Got it? Fine.

Although the tournament player will hit the ball 'on the rise,' this is not recommended for the beginner, nor is any attempt to give the ball spin or cut. The 'flat shot' is fundamental. So, too, is keeping your eye on the ball. Although that may sound a bit elementary, it isn't, believe me. Even tournament players, and I have been found guilty, often look where they expect to place their shot rather than gluing the eyes on the ball. Keeping your eye on the ball is the only certain way of hitting it in the centre of the racket.

Backhand? Let's make it smooth. The grip is turned, through the hand, one-quarter of a turn to the left. Then, you place your thumb up the back of the handle. For the backswing, your shoulder should be at a right angle to the net. You may let your left hand help guide the racket in the backswing, thus cradling and holding it in position until you are ready for the forward stroke. As the ball comes towards you (and watch those seams) you are looking over your right shoulder. Your weight is on your right foot and you rotate from left to right. When you hit, the ball is to the left and in front of you. The follow-through (the clock system) finds the racket head in a higher position than at the finish of your forehand drive.

The backhand is more difficult to learn than the forehand, but once learned it becomes a tennis weapon which won't tarnish. One's forehand may 'go off,' but hardly ever the backhand. Never, and I really mean never—even if it means a sure point—run around your backhand. The backhand must be a liquid stroke, no jerkiness, no attempt to put one's body into the shot, but instead complete fluidity.

The backhand is my favourite stroke. It can, if perfected, be a bold, offensive stroke rather than a defensive one. The average tendency is to develop a booming serve and a powerful forehand, thus relegating the backhand to a minor role. That's a mistake. Don Budge, the greatest exponent of the backhand, developed this stroke so perfectly that it became one of the most devastating shots in tournament tennis. And it never went sour.

Now, we'll give you a cannon-ball service, but before we start let's 'get the second serve in first,' to quote Alice Marble again. This strategy has psychological advantage. Your opponent isn't sure of your first service, but he's ready and waiting for the second one; perhaps he has moved in closer and now the psychological advantage is his. We'll move our hand mid-way between the forehand and backhand grips, letting our thumb lap over the side. This grip might be difficult at first, but I urge you to stay with it because the dividends have a high yield. Perfect co-ordination, and it's hard to attain, is essential; a feeling of looseness must be achieved and the rhythm must be flawless. Stand somewhat sideways to the net, put your weight on the left foot. The ball should be hit at the top of the toss. If you are tall, take advantage of your height. The ball should be 'slapped' and the contact made in the dead centre of your racket. There must be plenty of wrist action in your serve. This is the power serve and its reward often is an ace.

The primary tactical mistake is a steady flow of hard and soft serves. The power serve, if used constantly, burns up energy, drains one physically and is not recommended as a repeated first service, unless, of course, you happen to be Lew Hoad. Diversity is a keynote of any tennis attack, surprise is a factor which should work for you. Keep your opponent guessing.

Now, let's consider the slice service. This is one of the most effective of all, especially in the forehand court. The intention here is not to serve an ace, but rather to pull your opponent wide, out of court, thus giving you an excellent opportunity to put away a weak return for a sure point. The slice serve is just as it sounds—the ball should be cut as if your racket were a knife. The body is more sideways here than for the flat service.

For the social player, the next serve is not recommended. This is the American twist or spin and it's used exclusively as a second serve. For the tournament player (and who knows, you might become one) this service is a 'must,' for two valid reasons. Once perfected, it's safe and easy to get in; second, it is difficult to return. However, if not correctly executed, it saps energy and puts a strain on the back, Properly done, the back must be arched, the toss is over the head and towards the left shoulder. Bend your back to the ball and hit up. The more top-spin or 'riff' the better, as the ball will take a higher bounce, thus making the return less effective.

Never double-fault! It's almost inexcusable. You simply are giving away an unearned point. Don't foot-fault, either; avoid stepping on the line even in a practice match. A foot-fault judge may be lax or strict, but don't take chances, even though an added step after a 'big serve' will give you an edge when you go for the net.

Unquestionably, the most spectacular attack is the big serve followed by a charge to the net; then, the perfect volley for a sure point. This can be overdone. If you put too much faith in this flashy strategy your ground strokes may suffer as a consequence. As I mentioned, Helen Wills demonstrated that powerful ground strokes and a perfect back-court game can repulse and rout the finest serve and volley attack it's possible to muster. However, I do not wish to detract from the volley. Learn it, learn it well, but do not make it the cornerstone of your game.

Ready for the volley? Use the same grip as on our service. For beginners only, I would suggest 'choking' your racket a bit, moving your grip up about an inch to keep the wrist firm. Later, when you are at home with the volley, move your grip back down the handle. Volley strokes are modification of ground strokes, but instead of using a normal swing and hitting the ball you 'punch' it. Never take the racket beyond your waist. Stay inside the service lines, well inside, and don't get in the 'no man's land' of mid-court.

The volley should be used when your opponent is out of position, when the initiative definitely is yours. For women, I would not recommend an automatic charge to the net after a first service. Your opponent may be able to more than handle a hard first service. You should know, before you attempt a volley shot, that your adversary is not in position to make a devastating return. This is especially true in women's tennis, as the serves are not as powerful as the men's.

The smash is an overhead hit off a lob. This often is a sure point, although sometimes missed due to over-confidence and not keeping one's eyes glued to the seams. Never, never take it for granted that you are going to hit the ball, because even a slight breeze may mean the difference between a perfectly hit shot and one that is not hit in the dead centre of your racket.

The smash is really a volley that's hit overhead with the same swing as the service except that the backswing is taken straight back rather than arched. One must be in perfect position to 'put away' the shot. That means placing it where the opponent has the least chance of returning it. The shot must be timed perfectly, and if possible hit with power. If you are forced deep into the back court by a good lob, it's better to place the smash deeply and wait for a shorter lob for the placement. (Vic Seixas is a past master at this.)

When you're on the defensive, at a moment when you need a 'breather,' a chance to recover, use the lob. It can be effective strategy, a gambit designed for a tight spot, a change of pace. The lob, of course, is a high ball. It should be hit so that it will land within a foot or two of the baseline. A lob in the forecourt gives your opponent a perfect chance for a put-away point. Keep the lob deep!

Now let's play doubles, but remember the cardinal point: pick a partner whose game complements your own, a player who is compatible both on and off court. Two fine players working at cross-purposes are vulnerable, open to defeat by a team with lesser individual ability, but which can work in harmony.

In doubles, it's essential to 'get the net,' thus capturing the initiative. Get your first service in and follow it to the net. Always, and there are no exceptions, allow your partner on your left to take a return coming down the centre of the court. This, of course, gives him a forehand volley.

The time-honoured strategy of both players up and both players back still holds, but try to gain the net, hold the initiative. With one player in the forecourt and the other in the back court, your team is in an awkward and perilous position.

Fine doubles play calls for a perfect volley game, the well-hit return of service, the nicely executed lob, but more than anything else your partner should be chosen with the same care you might use in selecting a rare gem.

There is great pleasure is doing something well, and the good tennis player gets far more out of the game, both in playing and watching it, than the poor one. May I suggest that, even if you play a fairly good game, you take a refresher course? Obtain a good instructor, practise your shots, not with the objective of developing power (that will come naturally) but with the accent on making each shot accurate, easy, effortless and perfect. If a coach is not available, use a backboard. A week or two of steady practice will pay dividends when you start playing again. For the beginner, it is essential to learn the fundamental strokes before attempting a match. Trying to learn by playing means a certain groundwork of faulty strokes.

Good tennis demands grace, rhythm, co-ordination, and for good footwork I refer you again to rope-skipping. Learn to skip as a boxer does, on his toes in one position, then moving backwards and forwards.

It is a classic rule of tennis to play to your opponent's weakness, never to his strength. I recommend it, although I have violated this axiom. Towards the end of my tournament career, when I thought my game was at a peak, I purposely would

play to my opponent's strength. My thinking ran like this : if I
could break down the strongest stroke my foe had, she would
go to pieces, her confidence shatter because her biggest weapon
had lost its fire-power. As examples, Beverly Baker was better
off the ground than anywhere else, and so was I. Thus, I concentrated on her right forehand, hoping eventually she would
start missing a few and lose confidence. Louise Brough had a
big volley game. I've brought her to the net, taking the gamble
that my passing shots were better than her volleys. If your
strength goes, you've had it.

The hard, forcing game, 'going for broke,' shooting for the
lines is usually the winning one. Your opponent is on the run,
off balance, out of position, a victim of your steady pressure
tactics. In championship tennis, a cool and careful evaluation
of your opponent's game may tip victory's scales. There can be
a wide area of weakness. Perhaps you have greater staying
power; thus it would be better strategy to engage in long rallies,
wearing him down, using a safer and more calculated attack
rather than a more daring one.

'Getting the jump' can put you in a position of great psychological advantage, because some players are not good 'come-
from-behinders' and their games tend to fall apart when they
are trailing. I've always tried to play the first set as if it were the
last. I never took it easy in the first set or used it as a time to
probe or experiment. I tried to know everything about my
opponent before the match started.

There should be no rigid strategy, because the battle situation
is often fluid. A painstakingly planned attack might not come
off just as you thought it would. Be ready to change swiftly. If
a hard game isn't working, mix it up, diversify your play. A
quick shift to a soft game may be the answer, or perhaps a
mixture of hard and soft shots. Keep your opponent guessing.

Use the rally before the match as a testing time. Although
perhaps you have seen your opponent play before, he might
have had an off day; don't form any hard-and-fast opinions.
Remember, too, that, in tournament tennis, a fine player may not

play the same way twice. So probe deeply, hit long ones and short ones, watch how your foe moves, concentrate completely on his play.

In a match, make every effort to win the long rally. Here, psychology is a two-way street. Winning the point not only gives you a lift, but it gives your adversary a let-down, where disappointment and exhaustion both may take hold. Go for everything! Even the seemingly impossible. Sometimes, you can make a miraculous return.

When the going is rugged, the battle long and hard, when you feel as if you can't take another step, remember this: your opponent likewise is dead tired. The surest indicator of this is when no attempt is made for the extremely difficult return. Here is the moment to tap your reserve energy for the final bit of crushing power.

Keep your temper. No matter how bad a call is against you, your temper only will melt your game.

Pardon me, if I turned on the pressure. For a few moments I was back again on the centre court at Wimbledon. Perhaps I shall be there always—in spirit. It's hard, I suppose, to hobble a war-horse.

EPILOGUE

EPILOGUE

THIS BOOK should have an ending. My career certainly did. But now, there is to be a beginning, and my thoughts are in the centre court of Babyland. We are to have a baby in 1957. A tennis champion? A great horseman? We have ordered neither a special racket nor a riding crop. Our baby will have just a plain ordinary rattle.

There will be no prompting in the wings as our child grows up. He'll be exposed to tennis, riding and other sports, but he won't be forced along any championship trail. If he loves tennis, that's fine; he'll get plenty of help from Mother. But if his interest lies in rocket-ship trips to the moon, with a shuttle-run to Mars, we'll sit on the sidelines and cheer.

To me, my career was glorious. I would be happy to have a young tennis star in the family, but the burning fire to be the best—at anything—must come from him alone.

All we want is a normal, happy youngster, and we'll let him follow his own star in his own way.